GW00691894

Sled

a play by Judith Thompson

Playwrights Canada Press
Toronto • Canada

Sled © 1997 Judith Thompson
Playwrights Canada Press
54 Wolseley St., 2nd fl. Toronto, Ontario Canada M5T 1A5
Tel: (416) 703-0201 Fax: (416) 703-0059
cdplays@interlog.com   http://www.puc.ca

CAUTION: This play is fully protected under the copyright laws of Canada and all other countries of The Copyright Union, and is subject to royalty. Changes to the script are expressly forbidden without the prior written permission of the author. Rights to produce, film, or record, in whole or in part, in any medium or any language, by any group, *amateur or professional*, are retained by the author. Those interested in obtaining production rights please contact Great North Artists Management Inc., 350 Dupont Street, Toronto ON M5R 1V9 Tel: (416) 925-2051.

No part of this book, covered by the copyright hereon, may be reproduced or used in any form or by any means - graphic, electronic or mechanical - without the prior written permission of the *publisher* except for excerpts in a review. Any request for photocopying, recording, taping or information storage and retrieval systems of any part of this book shall be directed in writing to The Canadian Copyright Licensing Agency, 6 Adelaide Street East, Suite 900, Toronto, Ontario Canada M5C 1H6 Tel: (416) 868-1620.

The punctuation of this play carefully adheres to the author's instruction.

Playwrights Canada Press operates with the generous assistance of The Canada Council, and the Ontario Arts Council.

Front cover photo: Nancy Palk, Tarragon Theatre 1997, by Cylla von Tiedemann.

Canadian Cataloguing in Publication Data
Thompson, Judith, 1954 —
          Sled
A play.
ISBN 0-88754-517-3
I. Title.
PS8589. H527S53 1997   C812'.54   C96-931990-8
PR9199.3.T56S53 1997

First edition: February, 1997.
Printed and bound in Winnipeg, Manitoba, Canada - Kromar Printing Ltd..

This play is for my family:

My husband Gregor; my daughters Ariane, Grace , and Felicity; my son, Elias; my brother Bill and his partner Pat; and my mother Mary Thompson.

"Behold I shall tell you a mystery. We shall not sleep but we will all be changed."

— Corinthians I. 15:50

Nancy Palk - ANNIE, Pamela Matthews - EVANGELINE, Ron White - JACK.
— *Cylla von Tiedeme*

Contents

Foreword by Duncan MacIntosh

This, Judith Thompson's first play in seven years, is created on a canvas so large that it must necessarily be wide-ranging in its themes. Audiences of the first production saw it as a metaphor for Canada; a prayer for the dying; an exposé of the hypocrisy of life in the comfortable Northern hemisphere in the late 20th century; a lament for the loss of our natural language. It is all of those things. *Sled* is also a really fast ride, like our lives.

Making a theatrical collage of brutal and banal inconsistencies of everyday life, Judith has pasted truth and lies so closely together that they become at once shocking and revelatory. The scale of our lives today seems distorted and diminished by news articles, film clips, and sound bites. Judith restores the awesome size of a normal life in this play to that of operatic or Jacobean proportion. The characters, like those in Greek tragedy, are epic in effect, but rooted in dusty earth. And all of this is given to us through transcendent poetry and craft which she brings forward in innocence and blindness, making its power pure.

Henry James once called the work of Henrik Ibsen, another great Norwegian writer, "talent with glamour". If glamour means false magic, then I apply this description to the qualities of Judith's plays, especially *Sled*.

Sled's size, like Canada's, is overwhelming. Its horrors are the same too: implicit, only their tiny heads are seen before they strike. Omnipresent. Its redemption possible only from the hearts of the characters who inhabit it. Look for the ecstasy and fear in each scene — one cannot exist without the other. That is the riddle of *Sled*.

Duncan McIntosh
January 31, 1997

Working on *Sled* — by Nancy Palk

The relationship between the actor and the playwright is a very special one when creating a character for the first production. You have the person there who, for the most part, knows the answers to your questions. It's such a pleasure. And although some playwrights feel they should reserve comment, my feeling is "Don't be coy, don't wait for me and the director to come to it through our lengthy process, just give me the answer to that question and let us move on."

Because Judith (Thompson) began as an actress and understands the actor's process, she is usually a step ahead of my questions. For instance, I had some difficulty in "the Ireland scene" in that I couldn't understand how I could be playing Annie in a real scene — albeit a flashback — and then for a short exchange, be Annie's ghost, with knowledge of Jack's affair. Judith, of course, understood my predicament and was certainly willing to cut the whole moment, but it remained such a startling dramatic moment, the actual flipping from one to the other, that we decided it must not be cut.

I feel that I've learned to approach Judith's text by trying to simply get out of the way, particularly when working on monologues, to keep breathing, to try not to overcolour, or overindulge in any individual image, but allow them to accumulate one on top of another. The sense of momentum guides me and tells me so much about the scene, and the character and her state of mind. I often feel like I'm riding the wave, and the power underneath the text, like an undertow, is moving me through the play. In fact, *Sled* works most effectively when one scene rapidly follows another and the accumulative power of the piece is embraced. So, although I may feel the "I Am Dying" monologue is my 'aria,' it can only resonate after the neighbourly scene between Joe and Evangeline, and before Jack's quiet confession. I believe that *Sled* demands true ensemble playing, so that the audience follows the several interwoven stories, and then feels the impact of the piece as a whole, therefore enabling them to "ride the wave" with the company.

Playwright's Acknowledgments

I would like to thank the cast and crew of the workshop production which was presented at Tarragon Theatre in January, 1996: David Ferry, Carol Greyeyes, Roland Hewgill, Ann Holloway, Michael Mahonen, Pamela Matthews, Nancy Palk, and Maurice Dean Wint, as well as Kristen Gilbert - stage manager, Bill Thompson - sound designer, Alan Watts - design consultant, and Scott Duschesne and Jennifer Fletcher - archivists/researchers.

I would also like to thank Carl Mangialardo for honouring this play with his life stories, Pamela Matthews for bringing me the Cree translations, Robert Wallace, my husband Gregor, Tony Hamill, and also Urjo Kareda for his encouragement as well as his astute dramaturgy.

from *Aurora* by Candace Savage

The Iroquois people...imagined the aurora as the entry point into the Land of Souls, where the sky rose and fell into the world beyond...The lights were seen as the actual spirits of dead ancestors. Sometimes their progress across the sky was interpreted as a torchlight procession or a joyful dance. According to a circumpolar tradition, the northern lights are the souls of those who have died through the loss of blood, whether in childbirth, by suicide or through murder. Inuit shamans have been visiting the moon for millennia. Often the journey begins at night, under a full moon, when the shaman was standing at a blowhole, staring into the black, swirling water and waiting for seal to rise. Suddenly, he would notice a sled descending out of the sky. It would land nearby, and the shaman would climb on board. Once he reached the land of the moon, he might meet dead relatives or watch spirits playing ball in the northern lights.

Judith Thompson was born in 1954 in Montreal. She graduated from Queen's University in 1976 and then graduated from the acting programme of the National Theatre School in 1979. Although she worked briefly as a professional actor, she became more interested in writing and, at the age of 25, a workshop of her first script, *The Crackwalker*, was produced by Theatre Passe Muraille. Her work, which includes both radio and television writing, has enjoyed great international success.

Other plays include: *The Crackwalker, White Biting Dog, Pink, Tornado* - radio, *I Am Yours, Lion in the Streets, White Sand* - radio, *The Perfect Pie*, and *Stop Talking Like That* - radio. She is the recipient of the Floyd S. Chalmers Canadian Play Award for *Lion in the Streets* in 1991, and *I Am Yours* in 1987, and the Governor General's Literary Award for Drama for *The Other Side of the Dark* in 1989, and *White Biting Dog* in 1984.

She is a professor of Drama at the University of Guelph and currently lives in Toronto with her husband and four children.

Sled was first produced by Tarragon Theatre, Toronto, February 1997, with the following cast:

ANNIE DELANEY	*Nancy Palk*
JACK	*Ron White*
JOE	*J.W. Carroll*
EVANGELINE	*Pamela Matthews*
KEVIN	*Michael Mahonen*
VOLKER, MIKE, JASON, M.C.	*Derwin Jordan*
MOTHER, MARSHA, CARMELLA	*Ann Holloway*

Directed by Duncan McIntosh.
Music composed by Bill Thompson.
Annie's songs: music by Bill Thompson, lyrics by Judith Thompson.
Evangeline's songs: music by Pamela Matthews.
Set & lighting by John Jenkins.
Costumes designed by Sue Lepage.
Stage manager - Brian Scott.

Setting: The present, Toronto; a lodge in Northern Ontario and its snowmobile trails; a wilderness farther north.

There will be two 15-minute intermissions.

Playwright's Production Notes
_____

The play should run no longer than 2 hours and 15 minutes (not counting the intermissions). The audience should be out by no later than 10:50 pm, given an 8:00 pm curtain. The key to a good pace, other than in the playing, is in the transitions between scenes which should, in almost every case, be instantaneous — the last word of one scene immediately followed by the first word of the next. The designer, of course, can faciliate the speedy transitions.

Act I, Scene 1

*White birches, snow, a Great Snowy owl, and a
trail, with a hill, running around behind or
through the audience. ANNIE appears walking
fast and hard, out of breath through deep snow and
birches. The music is mounting, ominous like a
heart beating harder and faster but moving towards
a dark euphoria; ANNIE, walks the trail around or
through the audience and climbs the hill. At the
top of the hill, she looks down over the scene.
The music for "Oh heavenly time of day" plays.
She sings:*

ANNIE

Oh heavenly time of day
the snow and the quiet
the birch
white pine
so high and so high
Shall I sink in the snow and just lie there for hours
alone there for hours
till dark night
erases me?

Oh heavenly time of day

*ANNIE breathes in the air. There is the sound of a
wolf howling. She sings.*

ANNIE

lie on the white snow and
stare at the dark sky
the sky full of stars
who are people who died
maybe people I know

hello Maeve O'Hara
my mother's mother's
mother's mother's
motherrrr....hello!

A wolf howls. She makes her way down the hill.

Scene 2

A residential street, with mostly red brick houses with high pointed roofs, some three storey, but most, two-storey workers' houses. The houses, however, look as though they are in the middle of a forest. The birches remain.

JOE   *"America Bella! Si abbandonare a me!"* That's what she used to say whenever things were — fallin' apart. My mother. I don't think she ever said the word "Canada." It was always "America." *"America bella."* This here used to be a cow path. The whole of what you see now, of Clinton Street, wasn't nothin' but a cow path. My mother and father and the nine of us kids we were livin' south of College, that was about 1918, my dad workin' at the slaughterhouse at Clinton and Bloor. It's still there to this day, they won't move it; we'd come up here to the pastures and we'd watch as the cows walked down the cow path to the slaughterhouse, to become ground meat. Led always by the great black bull. Course we'd never see the meat, nor the milk, never saw milk till I went in the Air Force. But I loved sittin' on the fence and watchin' all these cows walkin' down. And all the Italian ladies, they would chase after these cows, to catch the manure they dropped on the way. For their gardens. And my mother, Carmella? She would be the first. She would always be first.

Scene 3

*The Lounge Dining Room at Pickerel and Jack
Lake Lodge. A warm fire crackles in
the fireplace. There is a trophy on the wall. A
deer with antlers. VOLKER, the proprietor, has a
German accent.*

VOLKER Good evening everybody. My name is Volker, and this
is my lovely wife Marsha. Welcome to Pickerel and
Jack Lake Lodge: The snowmobiling mecca of North
America. Marsha and me hope you are really enjoying
your stay and that you have seen the 500 kilometres of
snowmobile trails out there, and have wind-burned
faces, but now it's time to warm up, yes? So we have
brought for your entertainment tonight a great honour,
a beautiful diva, the sexy singer of Toronto nightclubs,
the very interesting and I think such a good singer, the
great Annie Delaney. Let's give her a warm hand, yes?

*ANNIE DELANEY steps out of the shadows in a
beautiful red dress with long red velvet gloves and
performs a simple transformation or act of magic,
as she sings:*

ANNIE Oh heavenly time of day...the fog and the quiet...
the mist
no sun
I move out of my dream and into this day as the fog
it clears so slowly away to
reveal...
to reveal...
to reveal...

KEVIN enters, interrupting. An awkward silence.
He sits down.

VOLKER   Isn't she fantastic?

ANNIE   I saw a fox this morning. On the green trail. The
long one? Early this morning. I was walking along,
thinking: there's still snow here. It's all melting
down there, in the city. Mud rivers running
everywhere. But here: snow, spruce, evergreens. I
was walking toward a heart-stopping stand of birch,
and I saw a fox. A red fox. We looked at each other,
for a moment. A wonder. At dawn; a secret time of
day.

My son, Jason, was born at dawn; that time of day
gives me hope. Whereas, the hour *before* dawn? In
the winter? The job that degraded day after day, that
picked at my being. It was dark when I rose and I
walked down the empty cold street and I am nauseous
just before dawn I wake up, with dread. My heart
beating very fast. I know I will die just before dawn.

She sings once again: "Thursday in November."

Thursday in November
at that duskish time of day
Walking west on Bloor Street. Past Italian groceries,
Korean fruit and flowers, Hungarian deli...I feel a
sharp pain in my knee a red dog, no, a fox, has bitten
me...

(*spoken*) It's a fox.

(*sung*) At Bloor and Bathurst my downtown
in the rushing
A red fox
Is here and
has bitten my knee and it stands and it stares back at me.
And we all

go down on our — knees on the spit covered
sidewalk and say
Oh heavenly time of day
ohhh heavenly time of day
A fox on the street
the geese in the V twisting this way and that
The lights through the dark clouds the blues and the
indigos, breathe in the chatter, the down to the
subway and buses to homes
See the fox on the street
grab a paper, a Mars bar, a *People*, and rest your head
Let the thoughts drift like I did on Pickerel Lake.
Just drift
Oh Heavenly time of day
Gives me some hope
And I do, believe that I'll stay
For a while
With this fox
On this street
A red coat
For a while
with its dusk
With its eyes

Scene 4

Lodge dining room lounge:
MIKE HEAD and KEVIN DORNER are eating
dinner at one table. ANNIE sits down and
immediately JACK praises her.

JACK   Beautiful. That was beautiful. Never heard that one
         before. It's something.

         ANNIE rests for a moment.

ANNIE   How's the dinner? Are you enjoying it?

JACK   Beautiful roast of beef.

         He offers her a bite, she turns her head away.

ANNIE   What did you mean "something."

JACK   What?

ANNIE   You said "It's something." My song. As if it was
         deranged.

JACK   I liked it. It was good.

ANNIE   But...?

JACK   You're not gonna get a fox on Bloor Street.

ANNIE   Well. I saw a fox in Trinity Bellwoods park once.
         Early in the morning.

JACK   You did?

ANNIE   Yes. I did. I told you about that—

JACK   Shit. Shit I forgot to cancel the paper. What a
             fucking idiot I am.

ANNIE   Shhhh, don't worry, Joe will do it.

JACK   Joe?

ANNIE   Old Joe from across the street.

JACK   Oh yeah, Joe. Ace.

ANNIE   He'll pick them up for us. He knows we're going
             away. He's my pal.

JACK   Why does he sit there watchin everybody all day?
             Doesn't he have anything better to do?

ANNIE   Give him a break, he worked like a dog for fifty
             years, he's earned his rest. Besides, it's great for us:
             He never misses a thing on that street.

                  He touches her knee under the table. She enjoys it.

ANNIE   Jack.

                  He takes her hand.

JACK   So I never asked you, what'd you do Thursday, did
             you swim?

ANNIE   Seventy three lengths.

JACK   You're amazing. But you like that, don't you, just
             thinkin' your thoughts.

ANNIE   Actually I don't think at all. I just don't have a
             thought in all that green water.

JACK	You are looking incredibly beautiful tonight.
ANNIE	To your eyes only.
JACK	You're the most beautiful woman in this room.
ANNIE	You look very handsome yourself. That jacket does look nice on you.
JACK	It better for thirteen hundred bucks. Hey. That was very wonderful last night. Last night you were all...
ANNIE	Shhhh.
JACK	I did pretty good with the hand last night, eh? You had, how many, four fireworks last night, didn't you? You are so unpredictable. My quiet woman.

He touches her. She looks at his fingers on her arm.

ANNIE	Jack? How long do someone's fingerprints...last? Say, in a house?
JACK	Ten years. Give or take. Less they're wiped off.
ANNIE	So if I don't clean, if I don't polish, my mother and father; their fingerprints will stay with us for ten more years after they...
JACK	(*nods*) Annie. I won't talk about hockey. If you don't talk about death. Deal?
ANNIE	"Behold I shall tell you a mystery. We shall not all sleep but we shall all be changed." I wish I believed that. For even a minute.
JACK	Hey. Look at the fire. You love fires.

At the other table, KEVIN, and MIKE are getting rowdy.

KEVIN   Sunday roast beef dinner, eh? Just like my old lady used to make.

MIKE   Right. Sunday my old lady would open a box of potato flakes. Throw some boiling water on 'em. There's Sunday dinner. I'm not fucking kidding.

KEVIN   Look at that waitress. Fuck, man, looks like she swallowed the Skydome.

MIKE   This beef is fine, man.

KEVIN   But where's the Yorkshire pudding? I want my fuckin' Yorkshire pudding.

MIKE   Yeah. Yorkshire fucking pudding.

On the other side of the room:

ANNIE   Is it working, Jack? This weekend? You think things are going to be alright? With us?

JACK   It's working. I haven't seen you like this in months. Maybe it's the nature, the snow, whatever. You're actually, I don't know, happy.

ANNIE   Yes. I am, aren't I.

JACK   Yes. You are.

KEVIN   HEY. WAITRESS.

MARSHA   Were you born in a barn? Or was it a sewer?

KEVIN   Sewer. That's good, that's good. You're Big Marsha aren't ya? Didn't you used to work at The Keg in Huntsville?

MARSHA	Yes I worked at The Keg. I think I tossed you out a couple of times, did I not? What can I get for you boys?
KEVIN	I was just wondering ... um, like ... did I fuck you?
MARSHA	That's not funny. I don't think that's funny at all. You're out of here.

MARSHA leaves their table.

KEVIN	I'm sorry.
MIKE	We didn't mean nothin'.
MARSHA	Everything okay here, folks?
ANNIE	Yes, thank you, wonderful.
JACK	My compliments to the chef. The roast is excellent.
MARSHA	Well thank you. I made the roast myself tonight. Chef was off sick, he's got some kinda kidney trouble. So Volker says "Marsha you're doin' the roast beef". And I don't cook, eh, generally, so I said, "Volker I can't cook a roast of beef." Volker hands me some garlic and some paprika and says "Rub it on, Marsha, like lotion on a baby's bottom." So there you are, it's not so bad.
ANNIE	Look's very good.
MARSHA	It's very good, I know. Hey. I meant to tell you, I like your singing. It's unusual. Different.
ANNIE	Thank you.

KEVIN   Waitress. Excuse me, not to bother you or anything, but like, we were wondering. Like where's our Yorkshire pudding. It says on the menu "Yorkshire pudding." Pardon my French.

MARSHA   That is Yorkshire pudding.

MIKE   Where? Am I like, buh-lind?

MARSHA   On your plate. There.

KEVIN points to the Yorkshire pudding.

KEVIN   THAT? You are tellin' me that THAT is Yorkshire pudding?

MIKE   No fuckin' way.

MARSHA   Yes, that is Yorkshire pudding. I made it myself.

KEVIN   Looks like my grandmothers tit, man.

MIKE   Looks like my grandmother's snatch.

MARSHA   That is it.

MARSHA exits. They laugh hysterically. JACK and ANNIE exchange a look. Annie is pleading with him silently not to do anything.

KEVIN   Look at those two, they are pissed.

MIKE   Excuse me, miss? No, you, big guy's woman.

ANNIE   Are you talking to me?

MIKE   Like, how did you get so tall and skinny anyways? Did you, like, eat the CN Tower?

*(Note: if the actress does not fit this physical
description, replace the lines with "How'd you get
so homely lookin' anyways? Did you, like, eat
Yonge Street?")*
They laugh even harder. JACK stands up, furious.

KEVIN   And that guy over there, he ate Exhibition Stadium,
        man.

        *They laugh some more, knocking over some
        plates etc. JACK walks over.*

JACK   Before we go any further, I would like you both to
        go down on your knees and apologize, to my wife,
        NOW.

ANNIE   It doesn't matter, Jack. Let's go.

JACK   You are going to get an apology. Do it boys. Do
        it now.

        Silence.

KEVIN   It's a free country, sir, I believe. And I would like
        to keep eatin' my supper.

MIKE   I'm really enjoying these green beans.
        Delicioooooso.

JACK   You are going to apologize to my wife and to every
        other diner in this establishment, or I will make you
        sorry.

MIKE   What the fuck? Is this, like, a Sylvester Stallone
        movie or something?

KEVIN   He's a cop, man. I see it in the whites of his
        fuckin' eyes. He's one of those, that shoves ya up
        against the car and bangs your head over and over.

JACK   *Diablo.*

KEVIN   What?

JACK   Just do what I told you to do.

ANNIE   Jack.

JACK   Everything's gonna be just fine. Annie. Just stay
                  where you are.

                  There is a long pause.

                  KEVIN and MIKE laugh and start eating again.

KEVIN   So as I was saying, Mike, I wouldn't fuck that wife
                  of his if you paid me a fuckin' million, like fuckin'
                  the railroad tracks, right? She likely smells down
                  there, anyways, right? Like a fuckin' can of
                  sardines.

                  MIKE is laughing like a kid, snorting.

                  *JACK slams MIKE's head into the table,
                  knocking him out.*

JACK   I have had just about enough out of you, you piece
                  of fucking trash — you fucking apologize NOW.

                  *JACK drags KEVIN to his table, forces him to
                  his knees and into a bow. KEVIN goes for his
                  hunting knife strapped to his belt but JACK pins
                  KEVIN's arm behind him, pressing hard.*

JACK   Now learn some goddamned respect.

Scene 5

JOE sits, rocks on the porch.

JOE   I used to have the satellite. Because I enjoyed the television quite a bit. Because I was a T.V. salesman at Eaton's for forty-three years. That was my profession. So I enjoyed my television. But since Essie got sick, I can't watch it no more. I turn it on, and I just can't watch it. Because I got to watch the street. That is what I am here for. Now that my kids are grown and gone. To watch the street. Trouble is, a kind of strange thing is happening to me. I'll sit here, sippin' on my coffee, and instead of watchin' out for how things are, right now, like if little Claire and Joshua two doors up come home from school on time, or if too many people seem to be livin' in the house on the corner, instead of those urgent things, I keep seeing: what has already happened.

Scene 6

Hotel room. MUSIC: sexy like Santana. Presumably coming from radio.

JACK and ANNIE. They start at some distance from each other and move slowly together dancing in response to the music.

Scene 7

KEVIN and MIKE in enclosed shack getting ready to go out sledding. KEVIN loads his gun.

KEVIN   Fuckin' cocksucker. I'll kill that cocksucker.

MIKE   Forget it, man, you know what cops are like.

KEVIN   Nobody does that to me. NOBODY.

MIKE   Well somebody did. A fuckin' psycho cop did. And it could have been a hell of a lot worse, we coulda been dead, he'd get away with it. Now let's get over it and go man. Let's go do what we're here for, we fuckin' risked our necks gettin' this sled, let's shoot us a moose!

KEVIN   MOOSE!

MIKE   Whooo!

They whoop and bark like dogs as they run out.

Scene 8

*ANNIE and JACK's room. He is asleep. She is
lying next to him, looking out the window. An
owl hoots. She sees the owl and the owl sees
her.*

ANNIE   Ohhh.

She turns, excited.

ANNIE   Jack? Are you awake? It's an owl, a Great Snowy
owl. I'm going to go for a walk. I'm gonna go and
walk until dawn. Wait for the light. Sweet dreams.

Scene 9

*It is a dark night lit only by a mass of stars. A
night bird sings ominously. We are looking at a
snowmobile trail in Northern Ontario. A green or
pink neon sign in handwriting overhead says:
"Pickerel and Jack Lake Lodge: Snowmobiling
Mecca of North America!" And then in small
letters, underneath, in a different colour of neon, it
says: "50 km. of Pristine X-country ski trails!"
The cross-country ski trail is zig-zagging through
a stand of birches. ANNIE walks by the sign and
heads down a steep hill. It is very steep. She
edges down it, grabbing onto trees occasionally,
slipping.*

ANNIE   All alone, in the woods, in the dark. In the middle of Northern Ontario by myself at night. I've never swam across Lake Ontario. I've never run across the 401. I've never driven across the frozen ice. But I am here.

> *She sings briefly in Gaelic. A shimmering, strange music. She sees a vision in the distance.*

ANNIE   I see her again. The girl. On the ship. A dark, battered, dying ship. In Gaelic, my blood tongue, say: *Long an bhais.* [pronounced: Long on vache] Big holes in the mast. The crashing of fifty foot waves. Maeve. The raining. Maeve O'Hara, born in Connemara, December 6, 1791. Praying. Standing on the mast of the ship. Praying to our Lord Jesus Christ. And everybody else down under, is dead. Of fever. Babies, and mothers, and fathers and families, all dead, piled together. They threw them overboard, one by one, wrapped up in sheets, until there was nobody left to throw them. Only Maeve, to say prayers for the dead. And she looks out to sea. For land, or whales, or fairies of the sea. In Gaelic, say: *Si na farraige.* And a cold wind comes up, cold and strong and she hangs on she doesn't fall but her hair, her hair stands straight up.

I know this is true. I know this girl is my great great grandmother. I know this girl is me.

> *She hears the sound of breaking branches. The shadow of a moose appears. They stare at one another for a moment.*

> *She reaches up to touch the moose.*

ANNIE   Oh. God. What is it? It couldn't be. Oh my God it is. A moose. I don't believe it. Hello. You are so big. Hey I'm not going to hurt you. Wait!

The moose runs.

A Snowmobile approaches. ANNIE stands, terrified in the moonlight.

ANNIE   Oh my God. This is all I need.

The snowmobile's light beams on her. There are birches between her and the snowmobile. There is a stand of birches blocking their view of her.

KEVIN   Hey hey shut off shut off. I see somethin' through those trees.

He shuts it off.

ANNIE   Hello. Hello.

KEVIN motions MIKE to stay back. MIKE keeps his sunglasses and headphones on. He is drunk. KEVIN moves in.

KEVIN   Well look at that. We got ourselves a she moose.

MIKE   Moose. Fuck.

ANNIE   Hey, fellows! It's not a moose. It's me from the lodge. The singer. Hey. Can you hear me!

MIKE   Shoot her, man, before she takes off.

KEVIN   Right cornered she is.

MIKE   Fuckin' shoot it.

ANNIE   No! No! Please answer me, guys. Hello! I'm here, through the bushes. What, are you wearing headphones? Take off your headphones.

KEVIN   Let's cut open her belly, and if there's a calf there, we pull out the calf.

MIKE   Where is she man, I can't fuckin see her.

ANNIE gasps and goes into shock.

ANNIE   This is not funny. Will you answer me please. Please. PULL OUT YOUR HEADPHONES.

KEVIN   Let's pull out the calf. Just shoot her, cut her open, and pull out the calf. Take it to a vet, leave it on the steps, whatever.

MIKE   Did you shoot it?

KEVIN   Just pull the calf right out. Alright.

KEVIN moves through the brush until he has quite a clear view of ANNIE.

ANNIE   My husband will kill you.

KEVIN   I want the antlers.

ANNIE   I'm sorry about the thing at the lodge, my husband went too far. He will apologize to you.

KEVIN   We split the meat. Shove it in the freezer, that's supper all winter. Moose and chips, moose and fries, moose and rice, moose and Yorkshire pudding.

ANNIE   Please.

MIKE   Why isn't she movin', man? What's wrong with her?

KEVIN   She's froze; in the light of the sled. She's froze.

MIKE   I can't fuckin' see her!

KEVIN *Ek skal skjota ther huortu i gegnum.* [This is Norse and pronounced: Yeg skal skeeota tear hertu ee gagnum.] Let's shoot her man. Right through the heart.

Two shots. Blackout.

Scene 10

> *EVANGELINE comes out on her porch and looks*
> *around with great expectation. She is looking for*
> *another neighbour's tame pigeons. She sees them,*
> *flying in circles. She follows them with her eyes.*
> *They make quite a racket.*

EVANGELINE   Morning Joe.

JOE   Morning.

EVANGELINE   See the pigeons?

JOE   Where? Oh yeah. A whole flock of 'em.

EVANGELINE   Have you noticed they do this every day at this time? Fly around in a circle, from here to the Loblaws over to the Food City, and down to Fiesta Farms and back.

JOE   Now that you mention it. I do see 'em flying around every day. I didn't think nothing of it. Don't care for pigeons.

EVANGELINE   They belong to a guy over on Grace. 'Parently he races them, down in the States every spring. They're in training.

JOE   Training?

EVANGELINE   For the races.

JOE   Well well.

EVANGELINE   How's Essie today, Joe?

JOE   I tried to cut her toenails for her and I couldn't. They're too hard. And yellow. Don't know what that means. I'm gonna have to give the doctor a call. Get that mobile foot clinic over here.

EVANGELINE   I could come do them later Joe. Before I go to work.

JOE   It's a nasty job, Ev.

EVANGELINE   Agh.

> *EVANGELINE looks at ANNIE and JACK's house. The house looks ominous to her.*

EVANGELINE   Ooooh. That house give me the shivers today. Looks empty.

JOE   Workin' holiday for Annie up north. Singin' in a lodge up there. She's a lounge singer. The two of them went for the weekend.

EVANGELINE   You know I don't think I've ever seen him.

JOE   Long hours. He's a police detective. 14 Divison.

EVANGELINE   So they're way up north.

JOE   Don't tell nobody though. 'Specially that nosey check-out, over at Fiesta Farms.

EVANGELINE   Hah. She's always askin' me when I'm getting married. Next time, I'm gonna just tell her "It's none of your business, you potato-faced grocery girl." HAH. That'd be funny.

JOE   I'd like to see that.

EVANGELINE   Joe.

JOE   Yeah.

EVANGELINE   Will you think I'm crazy?

JOE   No.

EVANGELINE   I heard footsteps last night. And the night before that. On the street. Real clear, like it was summer. And I thought I heard someone climbing the steps and coming up on the porch. When I looked out the window, I didn't see anyone.

JOE   Maybe you should get a dog. Although they do shed something terrible. Our Dory she was a piece of work; she would get up on the couch soon as we went up to bed. One night my stomach was bad, I come down for a Brio, I'm half asleep and I think I see my mother sittin on our couch. I go "now what are you doin' comin' back from the dead and sittin' on my couch in my parlour when you never let me so much as touch that precious couch of yours" and Dory she kinda whimpers and jumps off. Ha. Oh, I felt a fool.

EVANGELINE   Joe? Do you think, maybe, I mean, don't you think, there is some possibility that it might be him?

JOE   Who?

EVANGELINE   You know. Kevin. My brother. Joe? Do you think?

JOE   Oh dear.

EVANGELINE   Well, it's possible.

JOE   I don't see how, Evangeline. It's been 20 years.

EVANGELINE   But maybe he — found out somehow, about who he was. That he belongs right here. On Clinton Street. Like maybe she got sick and she wanted to just tell him the truth, people do that, you know, they get tired of keepin' somethin' buried.

JOE   Even if he did know the truth, Ev, what makes you think he's gonna come back here? This is not home to him no more, not since he was took. He was only four years old, remember. He's got a life there, wherever that woman stole him to, could be Australia for all we know, he likely has a job, a girlfriend—

EVANGELINE   But don't you think he'd want to come and find his real sister? And mother? I mean everyone wants to know their real family.

JOE   I don't know about that.

EVANGELINE   He'll be real disappointed when I tell him Mama's dead.

JOE   Evangeline, dear. Please don't count on him comin'.

EVANGELINE   I heard those footsteps. Joe? I know I did. Are you sure you didn't hear nothing?

JOE   Well...

EVANGELINE   You did? You did Joe? You heard them too?

JOE   More than likely it's just some drunkard comin' home from the Tasty's Tavern.

EVANGELINE   I'm going to stay awake all night tonight, and watch out the window. Then I'll be sure not to miss him.

JOE   Evy, there's no point in you losing a good night's sleep.

EVANGELINE He's gonna want to know everything about Mama, about our life before he was took. I gotta be ready. Tell me, Joe. Tell me about like, how she used to keep the house so nice. Before. Before she got sick.

JOE   She made apple crisp. That's the mother you should remember.

EVANGELINE She made apple crisp? With brown sugar on top? With what kind of apple, Joe?

JOE   I'm not so sure about that..

EVANGELINE But what kind do you think...like... MacIntosh?

JOE   Yes, that's what it was. It was MacIntosh.

EVANGELINE Oh. MacIntosh!

Scene 11

_____

Trail at night. ANNIE, in her red dress, lies in the snow before a towering tree.

Sound of an owl hooting. ANNIE slowly wakes up looks up at the owl.

ANNIE   This is very strange. This is very very strange. My heart is not beating, the blood is pouring, gushing out of me — In my Gaelic, *Vee a mer egg foil vache.* [this is the phonetic spelling] I am dying. I will be buried. Deep, unmoving inside a box under the ground, eyes never moving my tongue curling up mouldy inside my mouth these hands folded, living only in dreams, and thoughts, and hurried conversations in front of Steven's Milk, with dogs pulling at the leash and kids dancing round, "Did you hear who died?" or at the skating rink, flirting, buying hot dogs, "Did you hear?" less and less, and less, present only in my recycled clothes, hanging at the Goodwill, in the hairs I have left in the brushes all over the house, in my fingerprints which will fade in ten years, she disappeared; they the neighbours they will go on and on for years Valerie Pratt rushing her three children out the door at two minutes to nine, every day, for years and years to come, Joe will sit on his porch the Sikh men will deliver flyers to our door every Sunday and the kids will play road hockey and I will have left so little; I wish to leave more on this earth, more than I have, (*big raspy breath*) oh let me go back, to lie naked in the wet cement, to spray paint my name in blue all over my city, (*another big breath*) to French kiss the men lying in doorways and stinking of urine, to run

from rooftop to steeple, to stand on a speeding train
and r-r-r-rave (*breathing becomes more difficult and
shallower*) I have made such a faint impression in
the world a bird alighting on a branch (*breath*) I
want to go back and resume my life and just be be
be (*breath*) with my son, my husband, just walk,
breathe just breathe again in the leaves in the snow,
walk (*breath*) and the snow can cover my footprints
the blue light of the snow dropping bare feet on
burning sand (*breath*) the August humidity wrapping
around me, diving into murky lakes with weeds the
rough of my husband's cheek (*breath*) the smell of
his neck in the summer the breath of my child, with
a cold, (*breath*) the smell of his head his head in the
night oh!
let me resume—

Final breath.

She lies, still.

The owl hoots.

Scene 12

JACK in the hotel room:

JACK   Annie? You in the bath? You enjoy your bath, I
won't bother you. I know how you love your long
bath. I was thinking about what you were talking
about, my temper. Like my ... anger. The local
punks callin' me "*Diablo*." What I did to those kids
tonight and that thing with Pochinshky on
Eglinton. I was thinking — I have to tell you
something I haven't told you yet.

Remember, we ran into that — Jemma? The legal
secretary from Brantford, blonde with the moussed
hair — in February. Remember? At Yorkdale
Mall? And remember how uncomfortable you said
you felt? The way she looked at you? You said
you thought there was something...

I used to ... get very pissed at Jemma.
Sometimes I think it was because she was blonde.
And she was so big breasted. I, like, I wanted to
own her. I would leave you at home reading in your
nightgown, tellin' you I had to work all night and I
would drive to Brantford to see Jemma, to have sex
with her four, five times every which way I did
things to her that ... and then I would drive home
and slide into bed next to you and we would talk
that sweet night talk and you were so trusting — I
was an animal. I was out of control. I still don't
get it. I don't get why it happened. I didn't tell you
before because I was afraid you wouldn't forgive me;
maybe you won't forgive me, maybe you'll get
outta the bath and say you want a separation, I

wouldn't blame you. But I love you so much I
wanted to tell you the whole truth. I was good as
golden right up till I was nine. You know? The
perfect kid. I would give my dad the paper, ask him
if he wanted a beer, go get it for him, help my
Mama with the table, change my baby sister.
Sundays, I would put on the little suit, and we'd go
to church. My sister and I would get under a blanket
on the couch and watch cartoons all morning. I'd
talk French with my gramma, sing songs with her;
I played every sport goin', hockey, baseball, soccer,
everything. I slept with my football. And then this
kid, at school, he started to pick on me. Take off
my hat, in the winter, throw it around. Say I was
cheating in ball hockey. I never cheated. But he
was a grade older, bigger, and said I couldn't play
ball hockey. And I would sit there, on the side, and
hope to be asked.

It was around then, I got — angry at home. I put
holes in the walls with my fists. I wouldn't talk
French wouldn't eat French, if my mother put
tortière and sugar pie on the table I would throw 'em
on the floor, "You stupid bitch, I want a hamburger
and a fuckin' popcicle not this frog shit, not this
..." I never kissed a woman till you, Annie. I
would turn away. I would say, I'm not one for
kissing. Because kissing meant ... I don't know.
Being there. Goin' inside like an underwater cave
with someone, swimmin' in, hand in hand, and
you're under the water, inside the cave, with this
person, and so much so much could go wrong.
You're not the first woman I slept with, as you
know, and maybe not the last, as you also know,
but you are the first, and the last woman I will ever
kiss.

Annie?

Scene 12A

EVANGELINE's house. She is in a slip, about to get dressed for her job at Fran's. The ghost of her mother stands behind her.

MOTHER   Evangeline. My lovely girl.

EVANGELINE Oh Mama, I am so lonely. I am missing you so much.

MOTHER   I'm all around you ,Vange.

EVANGELINE I've been waitin' so long for Kevy I've forgotten how to make friends.

MOTHER   I can see him coming, like a storm, my love.

EVANGELINE My Kevin? My brother? Is coming back?

MOTHER   Oh. My lovely child. Just...

MOTHER is trying to warn her.

Scene 13

The two snowmobilers walk through the brush towards ANNIE's fallen body. They do not see her yet.

MIKE   Wait'll my dad sees all this moose meat in his freezer. He's always after me sayin' I never bring home nothin' he will go freaky when he sees a pair of antlers sittin' on his kitchen table.

KEVIN   Hey. I'm gettin the antlers. I'm the one that...

MIKE sees ANNIE lying in the snow.

MIKE   Oh my God. Oh my fucking God.

KEVIN   The lady from the lodge.

MIKE throws up and throws down the earphones.

MIKE   I told you we shouldn't wear these fucking things. Fuck. I'm blind in one eye, man, I didn't fuckin' see her through all them trees. What's your fuckin' excuse? Eh? Eh? Why didn't you see her?

KEVIN   I did see her. And so did you, Mike.

MIKE   What? What do you mean you did see her? What are you talking about?

KEVIN   Mike.

MIKE   What do you mean "Mike." WHAT THE HELL ?

KEVIN　　　We were gettin' back at the cop, right?

MIKE　　　You are saying you knew it was her? You saw it was a lady, man? Why didn't you tell me?

KEVIN　　　I thought you were jokin' around, man. I thought you could see.

MIKE　　　No!

KEVIN　　　We messed him up good, man.

MIKE　　　I don't give a fuck about that, Kevin.

KEVIN　　　You know and I know we followed her here. Mike.

MIKE　　　I'm tellin' you I didn't see her. I can't see without my glasses, man. I thought she was an animal.

KEVIN　　　We only meant to scare her, Mike. We didn't mean to kill her.

MIKE　　　But we did kill her. We shot her. YOU shot her.

KEVIN　　　We shot her. Right through the heart.

MIKE　　　(*pushes KEVIN to ground*) Why didn't you say nothin', asshole. Why didn't you fuckin' say nothin'? You want to end up in fucking Millhaven? Do you know what that fuckin' place is like? It's a rat's fuckin asshole, man, it's worse than any fuckin' hell in any fuckin' bible. I heard stories, man, see what happened to Kendal? Kendal got knifed in three days man, the place is a fuckin' hellhole. I'll kill you man, I'll fuckin' kill you if we get sent down. (*MIKE unpins KEVIN*)

KEVIN　　　Mike.

MIKE　　　What?

KEVIN	Do you feel it?
MIKE	What?
KEVIN	The rush.
MIKE	That's the devil, Kevin. That's the devil, shakin' your hand.

Scene 14

JACK walks along the trail, pointing the flashlight in various directions.

JACK (*passing close by ANNIE*) Annie? Annie? Annie?

Scene 15

EVANGELINE is getting into her waitress uniform.

EVANGELINE I like working the graveyard shift at Fran's. Because it's quiet. And people who come in, mostly just want to think. They have scrambled eggs and toast with butter, ice cream and chocolate sauce, macaroni and cheese. And always coffee. They always have their coffee. With cream. With sugar. They are very much alone. I can see it in their eyes. Looking down. Smoking. Lately I been thinkin' about things. Last things. Many people say they don't believe in God or life after death or heaven or hell but I have seen God. I have seen God in the deep brown eyes of the smoking people who ask for rice pudding at three forty-five in the morning. The Indians, teasing me, "Hey Apple", whatever that means, watching me.

And I have seen hell in their raw dirty hands. The boy prostitutes from Grosvenor Street. Talking. Together. Lookin' around the room, never resting. Smoking. Joking around with me. Want fries. Jesus Christ. In their voices. The way their voices sing. In the way their hair falls over their eyes. Sons of God. I touch their shoulders, sometimes. And in those times, I know ... I know ... that ... I have seen...

KEVIN starts taking ANNIE's dress off.

I hope Patty's working tonight she always has the best stories. She's got this great big family out in Etobicoke, like six brothers and sisters and fourteen cousins and her mother and father and they have these big, funny dinners. And the way she tells it, she keeps saying everything is "so fabulous" and "so hideous" and she is just so funny.

And every time after she tells me a story I think it's that much more possible that when I get home...

Scene 16

*Night trail with KEVIN beside ANNIE's body.
MIKE is watching in shock as KEVIN takes dress
off the body.*

MIKE   I don't fuckin' know you man.

*MIKE picks up his gun and exits. KEVIN
finishes and stuffs the dress into his jacket.*

Sound of owl. JACK walks into clearing.

JACK   (*off, shouting*) Annie?

KEVIN hears him, takes off, and hides.

JACK   Annie. Oh my God.

*He walks over to her. He kneels, he shakes her.
He tries to give her the kiss of life, sees she is
dead. He sees the bullet holes. He puts his coat
over her. He picks her up.*

JACK   Annie!

Scene 17

JOE   I was there. At the table, in the kitchen. Sittin' on the
boarder's knee. About to eat my pepper and egg. When
I saw my father killed by his own brother. Shot
through the heart. With the gun from the garden.
They'd had to dig up my mother's climbing yellow
roses to get it, it was hid, ya see, under the roses. They
had dug it up from the ground to scare some Irish
fellows that were botherin' them at all hours, askin' for
whores and for whisky. My uncle, he was sittin' at one
head of the table, across from my father, and he was
cleaning the gun. My mother, she says "get the *pistola*
offa my table." My father he tells her, "be quiet" and he
and my uncle they are joking around about this and that
and boom. My father falls back. Blood. Spraying out
of him. Over the walls. Over me. Her face. She falls
to her knees. And she cries: *"America Bella, se
abbandonare ah meeeeeeeeee!"* I still hear her
sometimes, just outta nowhere, I'll be bringing home a
bag of groceries from Fiesta Farms, or walkin' to the
bus up on Dupont...

Scene 18

On the trail. Dawn. MIKE is sitting, drinking.
We hear the sound of KEVIN's snowmobile and
we see the beams of its headlights. KEVIN
enters, the headlights lighting his way.

KEVIN   Beautiful night. Clear.

MIKE   Kev?

KEVIN   Yeah, Mike.

MIKE   What was that ... shit you said ... before you ...
                 shot her? That fuckin..."Ek skal"..what was that?

                 KEVIN laughs.

KEVIN   English teacher back home. Fag. Used to buy me
                 cigarettes, C.D.'s, down jackets whatever I fuckin'
                 wanted. Knew all these, like, ancient languages.
                 Said I woulda been Norse, like a thousand years ago.
                 Took me hunting. Deer. Taught me how to say
                 "Ek skal skjota ther huorti geognum" "Let's shoot
                 her man, right through the heart." You like that?

MIKE   I'm turning myself in.

KEVIN   What?

MIKE   To the O.P.P. First for the stolen sled. And then
                 for the manslaughter.

KEVIN   WHAT?

MIKE   You can't stop me, man.

KEVIN   I'll fuckin' stop you, Mike.

MIKE   Kev, look. It was an accident. These things happen
                   all the time up here. My uncle, he got shot in the
                   Kap — I'm gettin' married for Christ sake, Kevin.
                   I don't want this on my conscience. Kev. Come
                   with me. If we own up we get manslaughter at the
                   worst. That's nothin'.

KEVIN   You're not gettin' out of these woods, Mike. I got
                   things goin' on, things — waitin' on me —

MIKE   Don't play asshole with me, Kev. I can beat your
                   ass.

KEVIN   Oh yeah?

                   *MIKE moves to KEVIN who then points his rifle
                   at MIKE.*

KEVIN   I couldn't take the green paint, man. In the jail.
                   All the jail's a kind of green to make you sick to
                   your stomach, never seen another green like that to
                   make you feel less than a piece of shit crawlin' with
                   maggots, they'll put me in with the Jamaicans
                   again man, cause they hate me, the cops already hate
                   me; living with that green, a kind of green that gets
                   into your mouth, turns all your food rancid, I'm not
                   livin' in the green again, not because of your
                   fuckin' conscience.

                   *KEVIN shoots him. MIKE is felled. As he dies,
                   KEVIN talks to him.*

                   *During the following speech, the Northern Lights
                   appear in the sky, lighting up KEVIN and
                   darkening him, flashing across his face and body.*

KEVIN   Mike, I'm gonna tell you about the greatest sled of
my life. My ride through the Northwest Territories.
It was this friendship thing I was hired on:
promotional. I replaced the guy who owned the
Bombardier dealership I was workin' in Thunder
Bay, you know Pierre, he was sick, right, he knew I
was keen and he seen how I handle a sled, so he
sends me on this fuckin' ride. First off, everything
you have heard about the toughness of pullin' off a
ride in the interior of NWT is totally true. On the
other hand, it happens to be the most beautiful place
on this earth. From the Bering Strait to the Tundra
there it's like nothing you've ever seen, Mike. And
all that wind, and snow and nothin' like nothin' for
miles and miles and no trees and you are, well, very
much alone. But you're not, Michael, you're not
really alone, right? Cause come nightfall, you'll be
sittin' there, and...Mike? (*pulling out his hunting
knife*)

have you ever seen...?

the lights?

You know, (*drawing his knife across MIKE's
throat*) the Northern Lights?

Northern Lights on KEVIN, as MIKE dies.

Intermission.

Act II, Scene 1

The North. Under music, KEVIN is running,
breathless, away from the scene of his crime, on
the trail.
A light and music change. KEVIN, with his bag,
is in Toronto, walking up Clinton Street,
searching for his house. The ghost of his mother
appears, full of sadness, for she senses what
horror is to come.

MOTHER   Kevin. Oh Kevin. I remember the day you were
born. My water broke on the Bathurst streetcar, goin'
down Bathurst to Queen, and there I was, stretched
over the back seat; my waters gushing out of me,
pouring out, like a fast stream, over everybody's
boots and shopping bags. Well when the car stopped
at Queen I somehow got off, crossed the street,
everyone staring, staring at me and into Galaxy
Donuts. The front of my dress is soaked and I'm
there with the donuts. The chocolate sprinkle, the
sugared, the iced, and smell of coffee overpowering
and BOOM I pass out and the next thing I know
you're crowning and the nurse said she said she said
"would you like to feel your baby's head?" and I
reached down and then I pushed and I pushed and
whoooooooo there you were, Kevin, all wet and blue
and bloody and they put you on my tummy and oh
my goodness you had such a wise little face. I have
never forgotten your wise little face. Kevin? Ohhhhhh
Kevin. Please— (*disappearing*)

KEVIN walks up the street and stops in front of
her house. He stares at the house. He looks at
the next house. EVANGELINE calls out.

EVANGELINE   Um Excuse me? Hello?

                   He turns.

EVANGELINE   Are you looking for somebody in particular? I uh
                   — know the neighbourhood pretty well.

KEVIN   Yeah. Yeah I am.

                   *He searches in his bag for a notebook with the
                   particulars written on it. He finds it and reads her
                   name.*

KEVIN   I'm lookin' for a — uh — a woman called
                   Evangeline Melnyk? The street number got blurred,
                   right? But the name, I can read. Is there anyone of
                   that name who lives around here? Or did? With her
                   mother, name of — Crystal —? But, then, the
                   mother, I was told she passed away sometime last
                   year, so this Evangeline, she would be livin' alone
                   now. If she was still here.

                   *She is in shock so he doesn't see a response in
                   her face.*

KEVIN   It must be other side of Bloor then. Okay, *thanks*
                   for your *help*, have a good day!

                   *He heads down the road. She lets him go till he
                   is almost out of sight.*

EVANGELINE   Kevin?

                   *He turns, slowly. They look at one another.
                   They know. During JOE's speech, they slowly
                   make their way inside.*

Scene 2

JOE is at the grocery store. We see the fruit and vegetable stand. He calls in to the owner, and then walks home.

JOE   *Grazie, Vincente! Ciao! (he starts his walk home)* I don't read Italian and I don't write Italian. But I can speak it. Pretty well. I grew up speakin' it. To my mother. To the fella who ran this store. To a couple of neighbours. To everyone else, I spoke English. You have to bury all that. Once you're here. In Canada. My father, Carlo, he arrived at Union Station in 1909, all by himself. He gets off the train and he leaves the station and he walks up Yonge Street. What else is he gonna do? He sees a man selling bananas, he goes up to him he says "*Paesano,*" can you tell me where I might get a room, and a job." The guy sellin' bananas he's Calabrese, and he tells him he can work on the railroad for 7 cents an hour, or sell bananas, then he asks my father if he has a gun, a *pistola*, and my father says "Yeah," and then the guy says to him "Bury your gun." Like, in the garden. He tells him if the cops catch you with a gun, you're on the next boat back.

I speak Italian when I get together with my brothers and sisters, you know, a mix of Italian and Canadian, I speak it to old Annunciata, down the street, but to tell you the truth. I'm always behind, translating, back into English in my head. So I guess I don't really speak it. My children, they don't speak it at all.

Scene 3

In the sitting room.

KEVIN   Until a few months ago, I thought I'd never been to Toronto. I thought I was born in North Bay and I thought Diane was my true mother.

EVANGELINE   Kevin. Oh Kevin.

KEVIN   So she's in hospital with cancer last year and she calls me to her bedside and she tells me that she's not my mother at all. She says she had been my babysitter and she had stole me away from my home in Toronto when I was four years old. At first I thought she was delirious, right? With the morphine, eh? I didn't think nothin' of it.

EVANGELINE   It's true. She stole you away from us Kevin. We nearly died of it, the whole city was lookin' for you, flowers on our porch every day, hundreds and hundreds of cards, the police, the whole city—

   KEVIN goes into his backpack and pulls out a wind-up music box from home.

KEVIN   (*winding the music box*) Then I had to be in T.O. on business. And ... I found the name and address she gave me, right? So I thought I'd check it out.

   He gives it to her. It plays.

EVANGELINE   Oh Kevin. I've been waiting for you for so long.

KEVIN   I'd forgotten about you. And my real mother.
         Everything. Because I was so young ... when she ...
         fuck. This is fucking...

         An awkward silence.

EVANGELINE   And Diane, did she — Was she—?

         *He sees EVANGELINE is wondering if he was ill
         treated. He was, so he can't answer.*

KEVIN   Huh? Yeah ... What are the — uh — balloons and
         that for?

         *He is starting to get edgy, looking through the
         curtain out into the street, nervous that cops
         might have followed him.*

EVANGELINE   Just — your birthday.

KEVIN   It's not — Oh yeah?

EVANGELINE   March 27th. Didn't—?

KEVIN   No. She didn't.

EVANGELINE   You're twenty-four, right?

KEVIN   Yeah. Today. I guess.

EVANGELINE   I always wished you happy birthday. Every year.

KEVIN   Cool.

EVANGELINE   You're shaking. Kevin? What's the matter?

KEVIN   Crashed. Snowmobile. White snow, dark, and —

EVANGELINE   What, a moose? A deer? Kev? You crashed into a
         moose?

Scene 4

JOE is working in his garden. Sound of a car driving up to the back. Door slamming. JACK walks along the side path to the front of the house, with luggage. He ignores JOE and carries the luggage up the front steps.

JOE   Jack. How was your holiday? Still got snow up there?

JACK just stares.

JOE   Everything okay? Jack?

JACK appears frozen. He tries to get his keys.

JOE   I got your papers, if you want 'em. You forgot to cancel. I know what that's like, I'm forgetful too. Where's Annie?

Sound of robins.

JOE   Oh listen to that. First robin. First robin of the year.

JACK   There uh...there was...

Silence.

JACK   I didn't know how to give her the kiss. If I'd known how to give her the kiss, she would be alive today.

JOE   Oh my God.

JACK	They go into the woods. For deer meat. They're jittery, they been drinking, they been there for days, nights, seen nothing. They see a shape. They shoot. Guy told me it happens a lot up there. People get shot. Mistaken for deer, usually. Should never go walking at night. I told Volker, he should have put up a sign. It's very dangerous in the woods up there. Annie thought, people think it's like a...conservation area so they are safe. They think because they are in the woods, in their own country, and there is a warm fire back at the lodge, they are safe. They're not safe.

JOE nods.

JACK	There was...the poacher, he has something of hers, her dress, her red...I am going to find him, if I have to spend the rest of my life doing it, Joe. I am going to find him and I am going to tear him apart.
JOE	*Si abbandonare ah me.*
JACK	What?
JOE	I said if there's anything we can do, please, just let us know. I mean that, Jack.
JACK	Yeah uh thanks. I don't exactly ...

Silence.

JACK goes into the house.

JOE	*(an echo of CARMELLA) Si abbandonare ah me.*

Scene 5

> *EVANGELINE's house: KEVIN crouched on the
> floor of his room stares at ANNIE's dress hanging
> there. In his underwear, he sits on a diagonal from
> the dress in the corner, shivering. He puts on the
> dress. EVANGELINE is calling to him while she
> makes dinner:*

EVANGELINE You know what guess what? I was thinkin' we
could start like a business?

> *ANNIE's ghost appears. She is a little wonky, as
> this is her first visit back to her home and
> neighbourhood since her death. She moves
> slowly. She stares at her home with longing, and
> she turns and sees EVANGELINE. She sees the
> horror EVANGELINE faces, and she reaches for
> her to give her the strength on her journey.*

Cause like I know the ladies at the bank of Montreal
up at Christie and Dupont really well they're really
really nice to me, especially Gloria.
(*EVANGELINE becomes aware of ANNIE's
presence and stops talking for a moment*) I think if
we saved up my tips from Fran's, and you start
workin soon, we could save up and then go and ask
'em for a loan and then just start up our own
business. I was thinking maybe a bed and breakfast.
After all we have the house, it's paid for. It's got
the six bedrooms. Alls it needs is well, quite a bit
of work, but we could do a lot of it ourselves, hire
some students, and ...

EVANGELINE looks directly at ANNIE's ghost, and she knows something has happened. She is deeply shaken.

In his room, KEVIN is putting on ANNIE's dress. It is very clingy, sexy. He looks in the mirror, terrified.

EVANGELINE walks almost in a trance outside to JOE, who is standing on his porch.

EVANGELINE What happened? Did something happen? To Annie Delaney?

JOE A poacher. In the woods. Shootin' after deer. A terrible accident.

She stands, leaning against the porch, in shock.

ANNIE's ghost appears as KEVIN's reflection in the mirror.

Scene 6

JACK's place: He makes some calls.

JACK Yeah, Hello, is this The Bay credit office? I'm calling about my payment? Just to let you know that my cheque is in the mail, I put it in Friday. Yes, okay.

He lays out some clothes for ANNIE in her coffin. He lays out a red dress and shoes in the image of her body on the floor.

Meanwhile, KEVIN has heard from EVANGELINE about ANNIE. He looks out his window at JACK's house. He initially thinks of leaving, but decides he would like to stay. In the danger.

JACK   Yeah, can I have the number of the Bank of Montreal on Dupont and Christie. Hello. Yeah is Gloria there. Gloria. It's Jack Prevost. Fine fine how are you. Yeah. I was phoning about locking money in that high yielding account because my wife she she is in the morgue, on a cold in a cold her body is on / her heart isn't beating / a slab they are cutting / the coroner / her blood isn't running / is cutting to see the insides how the insides she isn't even thinking her quiet thoughts her quiet quiet—

He drops the phone.

Scene 7

JOE   (*to audience*) I ran; when he was shot and I ran out the door and for blocks and blocks all the way over to Yonge Street, where I found myself by the movie theatre, with the celluloid they used to throw out, after the show, I picked it up, rolls and rolls of it, put it in my pocket and I held it to the sun, so I could watch it burst into flames, it always calmed me, doin' that, I sat on the curb and held it and I watched as the fire flamed and then travelled around and around and into my pocket and fwoof I was fire, burning, red, my father, blood, spraying hot, hot and like it was like it — snowed, and white, holy white surrounded me, and it was white and it was quiet and there was only the smell of sweet bread. And then I passed out. In and out, in a cloud of white flour. Because the baker next door, he had seen me, on fire, from his window, where he was pounding dough, and he had run with a giant bag of flour and emptied it over me, over the fire, and surrounded me with his sweet-smelling arms.

Scene 8

EVANGELINE with a candle lit for ANNIE. She prays and cries. KEVIN watches her silently.

KEVIN   I know what you're goin' through. I lost people too. Blurry snowfall, can't see too well. I'm walkin' towards this figure I seen, on the ice, on the lake, hearing the wind, the figure don't move. I get closer and I see it's a man. It's a frozen man. His hand, like, out. Stretched. He doesn't look human any more I'm tellin' you. And I'm just starin' at him and then I hear, like a breath. And his one of his eyes, like was lookin'. At me. He's alive. And I look over into the bush and I see his sled crashed, and I walked up real close and I breathed my hot breath onto his face, to try to... he breathed in some air one more time and then his eye went dead like the other one and he was just froze. He was the frozen man.

EVANGELINE   When someone's dead they're dead forever. So long...

KEVIN goes to her and comforts her.

KEVIN   Hey now, don't cry. Don't cry.

His actions become sexual. EVANGELINE breaks away.

EVANGELINE   What are you doing? Kevin, what are you doing?

KEVIN   Givin' you some brotherly love.

EVANGELINE   It's not right.

KEVIN   Uncut nine inches, babe.

> *EVANGELINE throws him across the room. She is very strong.*

EVANGELINE   You are my brother. And you're in shock. That's all. You're not right because of your crash. So I will forgive you this once. But you must never ever ever do this again. You musn't ever.

KEVIN   Harsh me out why don't ya.

EVANGELINE   We're brother and sister.

> *KEVIN approaches her.*

EVANGELINE   No!

> *She slaps him.*

> *KEVIN moves away from her and sits down, crying.*

EVANGELINE   It's not right. It's not right for you to talk to me like that.

KEVIN   Not right, not right. Nothing's been right since she took me away from you, my whole life, nothing. I should just go and fuckin' die. That's what I'm gonna do, I'm gonna fuckin' walk right down Bathurst Street into the lake and I'll be outta your way and bother you no more.

> *KEVIN puts on his coat and goes to leave. She tries to stop him.*

EVANGELINE   Kevin please.

He goes to leave again.

EVANGELINE Kevin.

He comes back in. He undoes his jeans and rubs himself against her breasts until he ejaculates. [Whether this is seen or not is optional.] He then holds her tightly. She is confused. KEVIN moves away.

KEVIN Anyways, don't worry about it. It's not like we have the same father.

She looks at him amazed.

KEVIN Well, look at your hair. Look at your hair, and then look at my hair. Oh, by the way, I been lookin' over our accounts? And we gotta get you makin' some cash.

Scene 9

The North. ANNIE walks very close to EVANGELINE, and gives her solace with a touch or a look. The following speech is in rection to what has happened.

ANNIE I am a silent woman. That is what they say about me. When they have to say something about me. Oh, Annie, she's ... quiet. When she's not on stage, singing her quirky songs or telling her strange stories she is ... quiet. Jack, he really liked my silences. That's why he married me.

When I was a child, I would lie in my bed and hear the voices of my parents fighting, underneath me, night after night.
All their words like a claw in my chest;

I would go for days without talking, days and nights
and days and there was only one place I found peace
and that was ... under my dear grandmother's skirts.
A kind of chapel, there. Blossom was her name, her
real name was Catherine but they called her
Blossom. It was dark and fragrant under there, 4711
I think, lemonish scent, and I loved to look at her
veiny legs. Beautiful blue worms. Tea and toast.
Sweet wine. Falling asleep, together. She lived
with us, she spent her time looking out the
window, and doing watercolours of birds, and my
mother was always exasperated with her. "Mother,
will you just get OUT of my kitchen?" "Mother, do
you need to go to the toilet?" When she fell and
broke her hip, she was moved to a home for the
aged. It smelled of Phisohex and creamed corn. The
look on her face, when we left her there, on a cold
autumn morning, sitting on her designated bed. She
held onto her coat her brown coat and the look of
... there is no word; I stood there, treachery, looking
at the floor. A few weeks later, my grandmother
walked out of the home with a razor blade she had
stolen from one of the old men and into the
Rosedale ravine and she cut her wrists and she
walked and walked through the brown and yellow
leaves and she turned in circles and then bowed,
deeply, I think.

*ANNIE grabs the curtain behind her, or an
imaginary dress and wraps herself in it.*

Ahhhhhhh! Ohhh there she is. Waiting for me.
Huge. With her big skirt.......

This silence is perfect.
This is silence exquisite.
This is....

Scene 10

*EVANGELINE in a nightie, remembering. Her
mother's ghost is there, and speaks, slightly
drunkenly.*

MOTHER   Oh babe you woulda loved Nathan. He was a
dreamer, like you, always ... tellin' me his funny
stories in that deep sexy voice, wearing that tall
black hat, with his black glossy hair, long: Him
and me we made this seafood soup with the, the
shrimp and the whitefish and after we lay in the
backyard under the lilac tree...

*EVANGELINE walks over to JOE's porch and
checks to find him rocking in his chair:*

JOE   Everything okay?

EVANGELINE   I couldn't sleep.

JOE   Nope. Me neither.

EVANGELINE   Joe. Do you mind if I ask you something?

JOE   Go right ahead.

EVANGELINE   Did you know my father?

JOE   Sure, I knew Bert, when he was around. Worked up
at the TTC. Nice fella. Till he took to the bottle.
But that's not his fault, really.

EVANGELINE   And Bert was my father. My real and natural father.

JOE is silent.

EVANGELINE   Joe? Do you know anything that I don't know?

Silence

EVANGELINE   Joe? I always knew I looked well not like my mother and father but I figured I must be some you know, genetic throwback to like an Indian or Spanish great grandmother somethin' like that; my mother when she was drinking she used to say something about ... a man named Nathan?

Silence.

EVANGELINE   Joe?

JOE   There was a guy. Used to come around. Before she married Bert.

Silence.

EVANGELINE   Did she have me before she married Bert? Joe, please, just tell me the truth.

JOE   Bert, he didn't seem to mind. I always figured she had told you.

EVANGELINE   No.

JOE   I don't think she told the guy neither.

EVANGELINE   His name was Nathan?

JOE   Yes, yes I think it was. He was a nice enough fellow. Tall, with the long hair, an Indian fellow I believe. You know, Canadian Indian.

EVANGELINE   Indian? Oh my goodness. Indian?.

JOE   He said ... somethin' about he was teaching book writing at George Brown. He had a couple of books you could buy in the bookstores. And your Mom she was going for the cooking, to become a chef. She brought him home one night. I could hear the two of them laughing from two blocks away. Your mom told me they stayed up all night cooking and laughing. Oh he brought out the woman's laugh. She stopped laughing when she married Bert.

EVANGELINE   Nathan was my father.

JOE   I think that's what your mom told Essie.

EVANGELINE   (*touching her hair*) And you say he was Indian? Joe?

They sit in silence

Scene 11

JOE   After he was killed, my mother became nervous. She was nervous of me. Second son. Because she blamed me. Second son. For the shooting. She thought my playing with the pepper and egg distracted my uncle, caused him to shoot off the gun. And kill my father. Second son. The way she looked at me when he fell ... it is a look — I wish I had never...

Scene 12

*EVANGELINE and KEVIN walking down the
street. She wears spiked high heels that he has
given her.*

KEVIN   Beautiful. Remember: smile, talk nice.

EVANGELINE   I don't know what to say.

KEVIN   Don't say nothin'. I'll say.

EVANGELINE   Only for a couple weeks, right? Just till we get up
                 the money for the roof.

KEVIN   You're wobbling.

EVANGELINE   I am not.

KEVIN   Don't fucking wobble. If you wobble you won't
                 get the fucking job.

EVANGELINE   Well maybe I don't want the job, you bad-breath
                 pimp. Whoremonger. (*as KEVIN walks away*) I'm
                 sorry. I'm sorry okay, your breath is fine, I didn't
                 mean it.

KEVIN   You're tryin' to make me feel bad, aren't you?

EVANGELINE   No.

KEVIN   Don't try to make me feel bad, Evangeline, I'm just
                 tryin' to keep us alive here. Okay? Let me tell you
                 something: There is only one thing in this world I
                 ever ever did that I feel bad about and that is—

JOE appears on his porch.

EVANGELINE   (*cutting him off*) Kevin. C'mere, I want you to meet somebody.

They move to JOE's porch

JOE   Hello. Good morning.

EVANGELINE   Joe? I would like you to meet my brother Kevin. Again.

JOE   Kevin. It's a huge pleasure. And a very big surprise. Ev told me this morning on the phone and I almost fell to the floor! I remember you very well indeed. You would climb up our stairs and you would stand in front of the door and say "Open." "Open." Curly blonde hair. Essie would say "That kid is too cute for words." She'd laugh.

KEVIN   A long time ago.

JOE   "Even the fox must sleep," that's what Essie would say when we seen you sleepin' on the porch.

KEVIN   Oh yeah?

JOE   Well you've made your sister very happy.

KEVIN   That's nice.

JOE   Gonna stay for a while? Get some work?

JACK enters onto his porch for a breath of air.

KEVIN   I'll stay for a while.

JOE   It's good to have you back.

KEVIN   Even the fox must sleep.

JOE waves to JACK. When KEVIN sees him we hear the sound of the bullet that killed ANNIE.

KEVIN   C'mon we gotta go.

EVANGELINE and KEVIN leave.

JOE   Bye now.

JOE watches EVANGELINE wobble up the road. This reminds him of the past. JOE's mother, CARMELLA, comes up the road with a shoe in her hand and a broom.

CARMELLA   Joe.

JOE   Mama!

CARMELLA   I told you not to go climbing fences and playing rough. We can't afford another pair of shoes. What are you trying to do?

JOE   Ya can't get me a pair of shoes?

CARMELLA   We can't afford nothing. We can't afford a loaf of bread for the ten of us, Joe. You know that. You do this on purpose, to make me cry, don't you, you bad, bad..

She hits him with her broom.

JOE   Ask the priest, Mama. The priest always helps us.

CARMELLA   I canno go that priest again, Joey. I canno do that.

JOE   Mama. Please. What am I going to wear?

She is silent.

JOE   Mama.

CARMELLA takes off her Depression-era widow shoes and presents them.

CARMELLA   You will wear my shoes to school.

JOE   But Mama, I can't. I can't wear your shoes.

CARMELLA   If you want shoes so bad, you wear my shoes. Put them on.

JOE   No.

CARMELLA   Put them on.

JOE   NO.

CARMELLA hits him hard. He cries and slowly puts the shoes on. He is totally humiliated. They are way too big. He walks, with difficulty, across the stage. His mother is very upset for him, but cannot show it.

Scene 13

JACK dusts the house for fingerprints. They come up very clear. He spots ANNIE's, and puts his hand on her prints. (If the theatre is unable to do this just drop it.)

Scene 14
_____

Funeral music.

JACK   Thank you all very much for coming. Annie and I
used to place bets who'd get a bigger turn out at
their funeral. It's clear she's the winner. Annie, I'll
pay you later. Ummm, Annie, she was afraid of
getting old. And now she never will be getting old.
(*long pause*) I don't know if you heard this already
or not. Anyway, I wanted to play it.

ANNIE appears. Song: "My mother and father."

ANNIE   my father and mother
are getting old
I and my brother
were sad when they sold
our old house
with it's sagging porch
and kitchen mouse
and view of the forks
of the Credit River
we were puppies biting at their heels
now they are old
don't finish their meals

They were big bright so perfect
now they are old
not as happy somehow
not as quick
not as clean
can't sleep very long
they get up before dawn
sit in the dark
Watch the dew

on the grass
My mother and father are old
When I say good-bye after Thanksgiving dinner
They have tears in their eyes
so do I.
for something lost
Something lost. And gone.
Am I saying good-bye to ghosts

(spoken) oh no.

(sung) my mother and father
Are getting old.

Scene 15

JOE's house

JOE   My older sister, Annabella, married young, seventeen, very young, to get away from my mother. Niko, her husband, he was older, in his forties, but he was good to her. The problem was that he couldn't see. He couldn't see. And it was the depression. Who had money for glasses? And when she was crying in pain, with her menstrual cramps, eh? Niko goes to get her medicine. And he thinks he's gettin' like a Alka-Seltzer and he puts the tablet in water and he gives it to her. It was athlete's foot medicine. It killed her in two days. I'm playin' ball in the schoolyard, I refused to go see her in hospital. I didn't like hospitals. Her body looked so stiff. In the coffin. The ring on her finger. Her face ... with the terrible makeup ... her lips and fingernails inky blue. God forgive me, Annabella. *(seeing a ball land on his lawn)* GET THAT BALL OFFA MY LAWN. I'M GOING TO CUT IT INTO LITTLE BITS NEXT TIME THAT BALL LANDS ON MY LAWN, YOU HEAR ME? DO YOU HEAR WHAT I'M SAYING?

Scene 16

> *ZANZIBAR strip club. EVANGELINE as a Mother Superior. JACK walks in mid-dance and stands at the back, electrified by her. She directs most of her dance to him. She throws her garter to him. Back stage, KEVIN, in the dressing room, waiting, watches her and notices she is dancing for JACK, and is enraged. She comes in and covers herself with a bathrobe.*

M.C.   Let's have a big hand, gents, for Sister Fantastia, our Lady of Perpetual Love!

> *EVANGELINE gives KEVIN six twenties.*

KEVIN   Seen you flashin' that cop out there. I told you to stay away from him, Evangeline.

EVANGELINE   Are you coming home tonight?

KEVIN   If I see you lookin' at him again you know what I'm gonna do.

EVANGELINE   Shall I thaw the chicken? Make some chicken curry?

KEVIN   And another thing. You're not bringing back enough cash. You gotta show more pussy, I tole ya. Flash a little candy floss.

EVANGELINE   Go to hell.

KEVIN   The house is fallin' down, Evy, we need the money. If we don't start workin' on it, we may have to leave it.

EVANGELINE   (*after a silence, loud*) Ha! Ha! Ha! Ha! Ha! Ha!

KEVIN   What's do funny?

EVANGELINE   This. It's - it's - it's - it's like something out of
                 Charles Dickens. *Little Dorrit*

KEVIN   What?

EVANGELINE   You know, you comin' back here, forcing me into a
                 life of ... ill-repute ... but you know what? To tell you
                 the truth I love it. I love fancy dancing. EXOTIC
                 DANCING. Takin' my clothes off. I *love* the
                 griminess of the place and the men's *hungry* faces I
                 love watching them jack off to the sight of my
                 swaying hips. I'm Lucifer, I'm bringing them light,
                 and I just think it's so funny that you think you're this
                 bad dude and I'm this poor little—

M.C.   And coming up in a few minutes, the pure and lovely
                 Fantasia, guys, she is just getting herself ready for you
                 as we speak...

KEVIN   Are you makin' fun of me?

                 She looks at him, kisses him. Aroused, he pursues it.

M.C.   And now ... the temperature rises, the temperature
                 soars. What's happening? Are we moving closer to
                 the sun? Oh no, my friends, we have a furnace here.
                 A furnace named FANTASIA. Gentlemen, please will
                 you put your filthy hands together for Fantasia.

KEVIN   Now you get out there. And remember, only your
                 brother loves you.

                 *She leaves. KEVIN watches her dance towards JACK
                 and shouts.*

KEVIN   ALWAYS!!

                 Intermission.

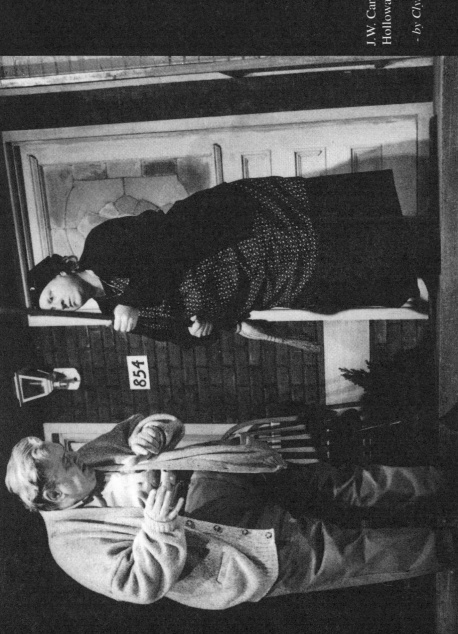

J.W. Carroll - JOE & Ann
Holloway - CARMELLA

- by Clylla von Tiedemann

Act III, Scene 1

JACK, in his dressing gown, remembers. He enters his and ANNIE's living room. She is reading on the couch.

JACK   I got us a movie.

ANNIE   Oh. What did you get?

JACK   A special movie. You know. Romantic.

ANNIE   Oh.

JACK   I think you'll like this one. The girl...is very good.

ANNIE   Ohhhkay. If you say so.

JACK   Listen, if you don't want me to put it on, just say so. I just thought something...erotic might be fun. Help me forget the shitty day I had.

ANNIE   No, no, it's okay. Actually I'm kind of interested.

JACK puts in the videotape. The porno type of music starts up. They watch. ANNIE is amused at first. JACK is also amused but the amusement turns to arousal.

JACK   Look at that one. The blonde.

ANNIE   You like her?

JACK   I just think she's good. She's a good actress. I
                don't know. She really seems to be liking...all the
                guys at once. I don't think she's acting. Do you
                know what I mean?

ANNIE   Hmm.

                *They both become aroused. JACK begins to kiss
                her. They begin to make love in an almost
                violent way. JACK cannot keep his eyes off the
                screen, and both times he looks at it he is more
                violent with her.*

                Suddenly, ANNIE gets up and covers herself.

JACK   What's wrong, you okay?

ANNIE   I just...I just don't feel so well.

JACK   Yeah? What is it.

                The porno music blares.

JACK   Is it the movie?

ANNIE   No, no, I think I'm getting sick that's all. I had a
                headache before.

JACK   Are you sure it's not the movie?

ANNIE   Yeah.

JACK   Okay. Do you want me to get you something? An
                Alka Seltzer?

                *ANNIE shakes her head. He turns back to the
                movie.*

ANNIE   Would you mind, turning down the volume?

He turns down the volume but still looks at the screen.

ANNIE   Would you...take it out, please? Take it out of the machine.

Take it out of the machine.

He does so. He puts it down on the table.

JACK   I thought you were enjoying it.

Silence.

ANNIE   All those men, crowding around her...

JACK   You shoulda said something. How come you didn't say nothing?

ANNIE   Their faces: dogs.

JACK   Oh come on. You were enjoying it at first. I know you were.

ANNIE   Crowding her.

JACK   But honey, it was what she wanted. She was the one that asked them all...

ANNIE   No.

JACK   Annie.

ANNIE   No.

JACK   Would you relax? It's just a movie. A sexy movie. Sex between consenting adults. What's the big deal?

>*ANNIE is silent. She is deeply distressed, JACK doesn't know what to do.*

JACK   There was no violence, I made sure of that. I just thought, something different...

>*ANNIE begins an activity she always begins when she goes into one of her silences.*

JACK   Please. Don't go into one of your silences. This is not a good time for me.

ANNIE   I'm going to go — for a walk.

JACK   A walk? At this time of night?

ANNIE   I need a walk. When I return I want it to be out of our house.

JACK   I'll put it out with the garbage tomorrow.

ANNIE   Tonight. Take it out of our house tonight. I'm not coming back till it's out of the house. I'll walk the streets all night if I have to.

JACK   Oh for God's sake.

ANNIE   Out of our house!

JACK   Alright. You go for your walk and I will take the movie out of the house. I'll take it right out of the neighbourhood. Will that make you happy?

>*ANNIE slams the door.*

ANNIE   OUT OF MY HOUSE!

JACK   I want to make you happy, Annie.

Scene 2

*The North. KEVIN is in the dark. In the woods.
In the spot where he killed MIKE. MIKE is
frozen there, like a statue. KEVIN has driven all
the way up north He approaches MIKE's frozen
body.*

KEVIN

Two and a half hours, 120 all the way, Mike. You
shoulda seen these bozo's from Quebec playin'
chicken with me I pushed em off the road man,
they're still waitin' for a tow.

*KEVIN covers MIKE's body with evergreen
boughs as he speaks.*

KEVIN

I can't believe they didn't find ya, Mike, fuckin'
search party probably walked right by you I'm
sittin' there down in Toronto thinkin' I gotta bury
Mike. He's my best friend in the whole world and I
will not have his body torn apart by wolves.
Goodnight Michael, I'll be thinkin' about you.

*He covers him up. ANNIE appears behind him, in
the same position as she was when he shot her.
He faces her.*

He runs away from ANNIE.

Scene 3

JOE and EVANGELINE on JOE's porch

EVANGELINE   Tell me more about my father?

JOE   Well, like I said, he was funny.

EVANGELINE   Funny? How? How was he funny?

JOE   Like T.V. Very funny. Make ya laugh out loud kind of funny.

EVANGELINE   Did he talk much about...his people?

JOE   He never said. Well, once he said somethin' about he could never do the sun dance. He didn't have the patience. And he said his mother lived out at some reserve in Manitoba. He'd go out to see her once in a while. I think he said he was of the Cree nation. I think.

EVANGELINE   Cree. So that's why I've always felt so — apart from ... Cree? Will I ever know him, Joe?

JOE   You may. You may not.

EVANGELINE   I just feel things are going in a certain way. And there's nothin' I can do to stop them. Like I'm in a sled, right? In a runaway sled goin down a mountain of ice, faster and faster and if I tip over I will break my neck and bones for sure but if I keep going, what's at the bottom, what's at the bottom Joe is the lake. I'll crack through the foot-thick ice

in a moment and down into the frigid waters,
stopping my heart and my breath ...

JOE I know the feeling.

EVANGELINE My very life is shaken, Joe. If you know what I
mean.

JOE Yeah. I know what you mean.

Scene 4

EVANGELINE's house.
KEVIN goes into the bedroom and looks out the
window. She wakes.

KEVIN Hold me, baby. Please hold me.

She moves to the window and puts her arms
around him.

KEVIN I missed you so much. I missed you so fuckin'
much.

EVANGELINE Hardly seen ya in the last few weeks, Kevin. I was
gettin' worried.

KEVIN That cop from across the street — has he been
around?

EVANGELINE Haven't noticed, really.

KEVIN Just hold me.

EVANGELINE Steer escaped from the slaughterhouse today. Ran
right up the street.

KEVIN Yeah? Fuck. What ... happened?

EVANGELINE They shot it through the head and dragged it back down the street. Blood all over the street.

                KEVIN opens the window.

KEVIN   Fucking — dogs.

EVANGELINE You know what he was sayin'? The guy that runs the video store?

KEVIN   What?

EVANGELINE That the earth is gonna get hit by a comet. Like, soon.

KEVIN   How does he know?

EVANGELINE The scientists, the astronomers have said, soon. What will we do when that happens? What will we do, Kev?

KEVIN   We fill up a needle. And we shoot ourselves into deep dark space.

EVANGELINE So we won't feel the quaking. The fires.

KEVIN   We don't feel sweet nothin'. Just like that steer. He's not afraid any more. He's not anything.

Scene 5

*JACK's house. He sitting in the dark, in his
dressing gown. He walks over to a table where
ANNIE is sitting, doing some translating.*

ANNIE (*Gaelic*) *Bhiomar ag fail bhais den ocras in Eirinn.*
[Pronounced:Vee a mer egg foil vagh den ocras in
Airinn] We - were - getting death - of the hunger -
in Ireland. I want to go to Ireland. To Connemara,
to look at the graves.

JACK Why? What for?

ANNIE I want to know—

JACK Who you are.

ANNIE Yes.

JACK You and about three hundred thousand American
tourists a year.

ANNIE Jack, I want to hear my natural language.

JACK They hate you over there. They have no interest in
you whatsoever. They don't see you as family, they
see you as American.

ANNIE I don't believe it. If I were to meet a Delaney I
know it would be...a very beautiful...it would help
me, Jack.

JACK   I have absolutely no desire ever to visit France, or even Quebec. Just because my name is Prevost? And my grandfather grew up in Rimouski? I have nothing to do with those people. *Oh tabernaque, je me souviens je suis tres* fuckin' *triste* and pissed off that Wolfe *il triumph de Montcalm* on the fuckin' Plains of Abraham and *je suis triste vive le quebec libre vive le quebec libre* that was my ancestors, on both sides, two generations ago, but that is not me do you ever see me watch the French station? No! No! I am this now, THIS.

ANNIE   I am going to Ireland. In the spring.

JACK   And leave me alone?

ANNIE   I need to go.

JACK   And if I ask you not to?

ANNIE is silent.

JACK   If I ask you not to?

ANNIE   And why would you do that, Jack?

JACK   Because... I would worry about you, over there all by yourself. The IRA is everywhere—

ANNIE   The IRA? Why are you LYING Jack you are a LIAR you are not worried about me being shot by the IRISH REPUBLICAN ARMY you are worried about me doing something that has nothing to do with you; the way you were with your girlfriend Jemma; (*she prods and hits him*) you gonna hit me too? Throw me up against the wall and then fuck me up the ass and piss on me the way you did with her?

JACK   (*breathless*) Annie.

ANNIE   You are just like the pathetic husband in the story
         of the selkie, the half-woman half-seal, terrified his
         beautiful wife he he stole from the sea would find
         her seal skin, her true skin because he knows if she
         finds it then nothing, not children, not love, not any
         amount of pleading, will keep her from the sea.
         YOU WANT TO KEEP ME FROM THE SEA.

         She collapses.

JACK   (*in the present*) Annie, you didn't know about
         Jemma then, I hadn't told you, this isn't fair, this
         isn't...

         ANNIE weeps.

ANNIE   But of course I knew, I knew in — here.

         She pounds her gut.

JACK   I even said I'd go, I said if you feel that strongly
         about it, let's just ... wait till my holidays in
         August, and we'll go together. What about that?
         Do one of those walking tour things you like.

ANNIE   No.

JACK   Why not for God's sake? Hey it's quite a sacrifice
         for me even goin' there, you know I like Trinidad
         and Tobago, or St. Lucia, I love to lie in the sun I
         HATE the rain. I mean Annie, Ireland is just like
         fuckin' New Brunswick. And who wants to go
         there?

         ANNIE glares at him.

ANNIE   You don't understand at all, do you?

         He looks at her.

JACK   I'm trying to, Annie. I'm really really trying to. I just thought if we went together, maybe—

ANNIE   I need to go alone. And you will have to accept that.

JACK   How long have you been sleeping with him?

ANNIE   WHO?

JACK   Whoever it is you are meeting there, Annie. This is classic—

> *She laughs.*

JACK   A lot of things are making sense now.

ANNIE   What are you talking about?

JACK   You're coldness. In the last few months.

ANNIE   What?

JACK   Like making love to a fucking corpse.

ANNIE   Go to hell. And fucking burn there.

JACK   You don't make a sound, you don't move. I don't remember the last time you gave me a back massage.

> *ANNIE turns away.*

JACK   What is his name? Annie? Who is it? Do you do for him what you haven't done for me in five years?

ANNIE   Jack. First of all, I swear on my life there is nobody else. And secondly, I am your wife not your concubine. NOT your concubine! If I am like a — corpse —

JACK	Worse than a corpse because you lie there and you send out these waves, these waves of like, hatred.
ANNIE	And that hasn't stopped you, has it? Maybe you like that, maybe you like — fucking a dead woman.
JACK	Get the fuck out of here. Go to fucking Ireland and suck your boyfriend's dick dry.
ANNIE	Aghhhhhhhh! (*she attacks, they struggle*)
JACK	Please don't lie to me. If you have any respect for me.
ANNIE	There is no one else. But I have been cold. I've been feeling — very — cold. I feel as though I may never get warm again.
JACK	And may I ask why?
ANNIE	I don't...know. I don't know.
JACK	Okay. Can I take a guess? You've ah...fallen out of — love with me. After twenty years. It's okay, I mean it happens. And I'm not exactly any great catch. You always much preferred the company of your son to my company, the two of you ignore me when he's here, home from college, maybe you're longing for his Daddy, your one night stand from where was it? The El Mocambo? I would just like to know for certain, okay? And once I know, I would appreciate the chance to to to...
ANNIE	Jack, Jack, it's it's listen. It's just sometimes I'm not sure who you are. I hear these rumours about you being a brutal cop, being called *Diablo* by the local kids and—

JACK So you're saying I'm like a stranger. Like someone you might brush past on the subway. Twenty years wiped out, like that.

ANNIE I'm going to work on it, I promise, I don't know, maybe if we go away, north to the country—

JACK My brothers said this would happen. They said you were too good for me, too educated, too — swish. I'm a cop from Mississauga with a grade twelve education. They would go "What the hell is she doin' with you?"

ANNIE No Jack, it's not any of that, believe me, our differences, I love, they kept things electric for so long.

JACK So what's happened? WHAT has happened?

ANNIE I have been having this dream. For the last year or so. And I am having it more and more. In the dream, you are walking towards me with an aluminum bucket in your hand. And in that bucket is a rattlesnake. (*makes rattle sound*) And I'm saying "Please, Jack, please don't come closer," (*makes rattle sound*) and you are humming to yourself and you keep approaching ... you have this rattlesnake in this bucket and I think the dream it is something to do with I don't know, with me sensing or my body sensing that you have...

JACK Secrets.

    ANNIE nods.

    JACK is silent. He does some cleaning.

JACK Well we all have secrets. Don't we? (*exiting*)

Scene 6

Zanzibar

Music: EVANGELINE does a table dance for JACK. Their eyes meet. They have connected in a way that transcends the grotty environment. She gives him a bracelet.

Scene 7

JOE's porch.

JOE I risked my life for this country! That's the thing. I was a belly gunner. In a Lancaster. Seventeen missions. It's cold, man, on your belly, you better believe it at 20,000 feet. They were always shooting at us, I shit my pants twice. It's the coldest I ever was in the belly there. Most belly gunners didn't last three missions. Because the Messhershmitt, they wiped us out. And the Night Fighters. I remember this one. We're moving along. And there's a Messhershmitt coming that way, and the other way. Well soon enough the pilot's dead, the second dicky's dead, he was a boy of nineteen on his second mission, and the nose gunner's dead. (*taking a moment to recover from the memory*) When the war was over I come back to Toronto. And Eatons, they got signs up everywhere 'We want vets'. 'Vets please apply.' Well I went down to apply, with a few of my buddies, other vets. We filled out the application. And under religion, I put Catholic. Because I was. Well all the other vets I knew, they were Protestant. They all got the job, right off. They were called the next day. I didn't get any calls, nothing. I said to one, "I wonder how come I never got called." He looked at me, he says, "You didn't say you were Catholic?" "Well, yes," I says. He says "You'll never get a job if you're Catholic. Not in Toronto. Not in Ontario." So I went to an Anglican priest and I told him my predicament. I told him I wanted to change religions and he was very accommodating. He made me an Anglican. So I went back down, and I filled out the form again. And this time where it said "Religion" I wrote down Anglican. And I got the job the next day. But to tell you the truth, although I was an Anglican, I was still a Catholic. You always are.

Scene 8

A piano bar at night with cocktails.

JACK How how did you think up a dance like that? 'Cause that is really exotic.

EVANGELINE Oh. I don't know. I just got bored with the same old thing.

JACK So you came up with this?

EVANGELINE You think it's okay?

JACK It's ... enchanting.

EVANGELINE It's a kind of a ...

JACK What?

EVANGELINE Nothing.

JACK   No, what were you going to say?

EVANGELINE   Prayer. In a way. You think I'm crazy.

JACK   No, I don't. I think that's cool. I pray too. By driving fast. Seriously. In a chase. Chasin' some guy who's just robbed a bank, or knocked down a kid, hit and run. It's like a prayer.

EVANGELINE   Because the other kind of prayer, on your knees and putting your palms together? And repeating words you learned in Sunday school? Those don't work.

JACK   I know, I used to try it. Please GOD make my brother get run over by a truck so my dad and I can get Swiss Chalet Christmas dinner. Please GOD let the guy not have a gun on him, please GOD let my wife have a heartbeat. It never—

EVANGELINE   You okay? You're trembling, aren't you? Here, let me—

She puts her jacket on him.

JACK   They should turn the goddamn heat up in here. What are they trying to do, freeze us out?

She is silent.

JACK   So how do you like the boss, is he okay? I heard this one he doesn't treat the girls so well.

EVANGELINE   No.

JACK   Well...do you...like working there?

EVANGELINE laughs.

EVANGELINE   You're asking me if I like working there?

JACK   Isn't there ... isn't there ... anything else that you wanted to do? With your life?

       She turns to him. There is so much to say that there is not much point in saying anything.

JACK   So why do you stay there?

EVANGELINE You don't understand.

       EVANGELINE smiles.

EVANGELINE I've seen you. You live in my neighbourhood.

JACK   Where do you live?

EVANGELINE Clinton just south of Dupont.

JACK   Oh. That's close to me. I'm closer to Follis.

EVANGELINE You're a policeman.

JACK   Is that bad?

EVANGELINE Your wife. Annie Delaney. The singer.

JACK   Yeah.

EVANGELINE "As a hart yearns for channels of water, so my soul yearns for thee."

JACK   Oh you've heard Annie's— (*EVANGELINE nods*) It's hard at night. (*ANNIE's ghost enters*) Sometimes I just get up, go out, for a walk. Sit in some all-night donut place. Keep away the thoughts.

EVANGELINE I know what that's like.

JACK   At work, and at the bar, I can almost forget, you know, distracted. But as soon as I get home.

EVANGELINE   Yeah.

JACK   Get into bed. That bed. It's like...I swear to God I've seen her. In the house.

EVANGELINE   I've seen my mother.

JACK   Yeah?

EVANGELINE   You loved her. Annie Delaney.

                      Silence. EVANGELINE nods, smiles.

JACK   Annie would have liked you. She would have liked you a lot.

EVANGELINE   I said "Hi." to her a few times on the sidewalk. We even talked about the weather. Our gardens. You think so?

JACK   Yeah.

                      EVANGELINE caresses his face.

EVANGELINE   I like those lines from the ends of your eyes.

JACK   You do? I hate them. Reminds me I'm getting old. Hey. Am I too old for you?

                      EVANGELINE is embarrassed.

JACK   Because I would like to, I don't know. Hang out with you. Go to the Botanical Gardens, you ever been to the Botanical Gardens?

                      EVANGELINE shakes her head.

JACK   Oh you'll love the Botanical Gardens.

> *EVANGELINE kisses him. He kisses her back.*

JACK   Do you mind if I tell you, I find you very beautiful?

EVANGELINE Me?

JACK   And mysterious. A forest. In winter.

EVANGELINE No.

JACK   Would you like to dance?

> *He touches her, caresses her.*

> *The ghost ANNIE sings. They dance to ANNIE's music. They dance politely, and then more and more sensually.*

Scene 9
_____

> *Song: "morning in bright fall."*

ANNIE   A morning in bright fall
In Caledon Hills

Maple leaves my bouquet
I had chills

On my day (*pause*)
from my lips to my knees
Love (*small pause*)
You were stung by a bumblebee
the ringing of bells
Your cheek swelled
as you said (*pause*)

Till death us do part
Clear eyes and clean consciences
Oh when did this start
This painful infection (*pause*)
Of our strong our red heart?

Oh when did this start?
Are, (*tiny pause*) we so far apart? (*pause*)

That morning in bright fall
Maple leaves — my bouquet
You were my prince
And now what you say
Makes me sad (*pause*)
Makes me fear

You said you were the sun dear
And I was the sky
But are you the gun dear
I carry inside?
Waiting to fire
To kill your tall bride

Oh when did this start
Are we so far apart
Are we so far apart?

Scene 10

*Dawn breaks. JACK and EVAGELINE are on
Clinton Street, looking at the stars.*

JACK   You see that there? That's the North Star.

EVANGELINE *Keeweetinok Atchak.* In Cree. I'm half Cree.

JACK   Yeah?

EVANGELINE	That star stays still. The other stars, they swirl around but that one stays just still.
JACK	You know it.
EVANGELINE	I studied the stars. The stars and some Cree. Songs, a few phrases. I got books from the library.
JACK	Wow. I like that, I like it that you studied the stars, and the Cree, that's elegant.
EVANGELINE	Your eyes — like a sea of glass.

> *She laughs, and kisses him. From inside, KEVIN sees, and, drunk, wanders out.*

KEVIN	What the hell are you doing, Evangeline?

> *They start and turn.*

EVANGELINE	You'd better go.
JACK	Who are you? Are you the brother?
KEVIN	Who the fuck are you?
EVANGELINE	Kev, please.
JACK	Jack, pleased to meet you. I'm just walking Evangeline home.
KEVIN	You come near her again and I'll kill you. Now get the fuck off my property.
JACK	Is this your house?
EVANGELINE	Kevy please don't talk to my friend that way. He's been very nice to me.
KEVIN	Get offa my property. Fuckin' now.

JACK   Evangeline is an adult, Kevin. And what she does is none of your business.

KEVIN   Evy, get inside.

EVANGELINE I can do what I want to do, Kev. You can't stop me anymore.

KEVIN   I said GET INSIDE.

JACK   Hey you don't —

KEVIN hits her. JACK hits him. They fight. KEVIN is trying to escape JACK and the fight moves inside, and towards KEVIN's bedroom. EVANGELINE tries to stop them, crying "Please." "Stop it." and "Don't." They are there, squaring off, when JACK sees the red dress hanging in KEVIN's room. He looks back at KEVIN, and back again at the dress. He touches the dress. They freeze.

JACK   Annie!

He turns to KEVIN. KEVIN laughs.

KEVIN   We thought she was an animal, man.

EVANGELINE Kevin?

KEVIN   We couldn't see through the branches. In the dark. It happens.

JACK attacks KEVIN hard.

EVANGELINE No. Stop it. Stop it you two, I'll call the cops. Stop it, You're hurting him.

They are fighting, JACK is about to kill KEVIN, by strangling him. EVANGELINE grabs the gun.

EVANGELINE   Stop it or I'll shoot. I swear to God I'll shoot.

EVANGELINE has a moment of terrible indecision, but then her need for her brother, for family, wins out and she kills JACK. The sound of the bullet is naturalistic this time, to avoid comic melodrama. He falls to the ground. MUSIC should come in right away.

KEVIN gets up, takes the gun, then steals the money out of JACK's pockets and takes off.

EVANGELINE has blood all over her hands. She is in shock. She puts on the red dress. She sings a Cree song of lamentation over JACK's body (see music for "Evangeline's Lament" at end of play.

She walks outside. JOE sees her.

EVANGELINE   Help me.

JOE   What happened? What happened child?

EVANGELINE staggers down Clinton Street.

Scene 11

Night. KEVIN appears out of JOE's front door, rifling through ESSIE's purse and throwing it away. JOE is on the porch.

JOE   Who's that? Who's there?

KEVIN	Cover your face. Cover your face or I fuckin' kill you.
JOE	My wife is not well. Please don't hurt her. You can have anything you want.
KEVIN	Shut the fuck up, Joe.
JOE	Kevin. What are you doing here? Where's Evangeline?
KEVIN	Where's your wallet? Where is your fuckin' wallet, old man.
JOE	It's okay. Now calm down Kevin, you're welcome to anything you want. It's right here, in my jacket.
KEVIN	Okay, now what's your PIN number? Tell me the wrong one, I come back and shoot your fuckin' head off.
JOE	Okay. It's — uh ... 6?
KEVIN	NOW. NOW!
JOE	6...5, no 4...no, 5, 7, 9. Yes, that's it.
KEVIN	6579.
JOE	Kevin? It's not too late to give yourself up.
KEVIN	Are you tellin' me what to fuckin do? YOU, who sat on your fuckin' porch and watched as I was dragged away from my home only four years old? You sat and you rocked and you didn't do nothing. You didn't do nothing.
JOE	Kevin.

KEVIN	I remember the sound of the chair. The sound of the rocking I remember it, man, I have nightmares.
JOE	I thought she was takin' you down to Christie Pits, to play on the big airplane. You loved that big airplane.
KEVIN	Bullshit.
JOE	It's God's truth.
KEVIN	Bullshit.

> *KEVIN goes to leave.*

JOE	Kevin. May God forgive you.
KEVIN	Fuck that.

> *KEVIN leaves.*

Scene 12

> *Night. Bloor Street. Fruit and vegetable stand. Streetlight shines on it. EVANGELINE is standing still among the fruit and vegetables. We can see Honest Ed's neon signs flashing across the street.*

EVANGELINE *(whispers)* Hail Oh Hail Annie full of Grace we are soaked we are soaked in our neighbour's blood my brother and I the Law the Law is with thee. Come to me I wait here, behind the apples and avocados and oranges sweet I will wait for you to to guide me are you here? Are you—

> *ANNIE appears.*

EVANGELINE Annie. Hey. Have you come to smote me down? I wouldn't blame you. I am murder see my hands? *Geen-sa. Ni nipbo.* [I have killed somebody. I am death] Soaked in blood His blood —

ANNIE Evangeline, walk.

EVANGELINE Walk?

ANNIE swings around and points north.

ANNIE *Keeweetinok Atchak.* The North Star to the northern star walk you'll reach the dark forest where the air is clear you lie on the moss you will have your baby on moss not a grimy jail floor; clean your baby with clear water not infected jail water you go, and walk and disappear. It happens in Canada all the time, a disappearing woman, nobody minds. Just walk. Disappear.

EVANGELINE Oh. Annie. Will you ever sing to me again?

ANNIE disappears.

EVANGELINE You know my baby? I'm callin' her after you, Annie.

EVANGELINE fills her bag with oranges and apples. KEVIN, meanwhile, is all over the neighbourhood looking for her.

KEVIN We gotta take off, babe, cause they're comin' after us. There's buses every hour we can be outta here in twenty minutes.

She starts to walk up the street.

EVANGELINE We are walking.

KEVIN   Walking? (*pausing and watching her walk*) Walking.
               *They walk together into the horizon, up Yonge
               Street.*

               *We see JOE's rocking chair, a yellow police
               ribbon around EVANGELINE's house. About
               halfway through the speech we see KEVIN and
               EVANGELINE, in the woods, in a sled or on a
               stump. He seems to be sleeping, in a sleeping
               bag beside her. She is heavily pregnant.*

EVANGELINE   *Tansi niskneeksqueem* [hello my daughter] dear my
               darling daughter.

               Happy eighth birthday Annie Northstar. *Kisageetin
               ooma* that means I love you, baby, in Cree; the
               language of your blood I hope this finds you happy
               and strong. My dear friend Patty is giving you this
               letter. Patty is your mother now and I know she is
               tellin' you funny stories and bringing home rice
               pudding from Fran's for ya, and taking real good
               care of you. I wanted more than life itself to keep
               you, love, but I had to send you down to Patty to
               keep you safe, because I am doomed to walk,
               forever. And that's no way for you to live. Your
               feet would get tired. I want you to have school, and
               friends, and gymnastic classes and all of that I do
               not know what lies ahead, on my travels. I know
               one thing only, and that is that you will see me, in
               the North Star, because, the North Star, in Cree:
               "*kewe tinok atchak*," is always there in the sky,
               Annie, and guides us.

               Nell, whatever people may tell you about your
               father, I want you to know that what you are is a
               long summer evening, Nell, Clinton Street, kids
               playing outside our window my friend Joe cutting
               his roses, talking with the neighbours, and we lined
               up barefoot for soft ice cream and Kevin he got a
               vanilla with the hot chocolate dip and I got the

warm butterscotch and we brought them inside and we sat in the dark and we licked them faster and as the ice cream melted his face melted too, melted along with the ice cream we had no fans, Nell our house was so hot, and the laughing boy was there underneath, that boy who said park and I saw him again and he was gentle and sweet and your father, my love, was not the man but the sweet heavenly child.

Kisageetin ooma, I love you so, *kisageetin ooma*.

Scene 13

EVANGELINE Oh I wish I could be near you, Annie, while you read this, touching the lights in your soft hair, wish it were possible but I know that it isn't, for the bone in the air it has broke I am doomed to walk till I cannot walk more till I fall on my knees to the ground till I fall on my—

Kisageetin ooma, I love you so, *kisageetin ooma kisageetin ooma kisageetin ooma*

daughter

Kev? Kev, come on, wake up.

KEVIN Leave me alone. I gotta sleep.

EVANGELINE Kevin it's time. We have to walk.

KEVIN Fuckin' cold, fuckin' wolves, howlin' in my ear —

EVANGELINE You're going to be fine. Come on.

They walk together for a while along the trail. They struggle.

KEVIN   My foot is killin' me, Ev. I can't fuckin' walk no
               more. Don't make me, don't—

               He falls.

EVANGELINE   No resting, Kevin. If we rest we fall into the fires!
               We burn. Forever. Now come on. You can do it.
               Come on. Stand. Up. Now. One foot in front of
               the other. Come on.

               She tries to make him walk, like a puppet.

KEVIN   Have some mercy, woman. Mer-cy. Can't you see
               I'm dyin' here? I'm goin' blind. Left eye is worse.
               Everything's startin' to look shimmery. Just the
               way it happened with the right one,

               He buckles.

EVANGELINE   Keeeevin!!

KEVIN   And the cold. Ev. I can't take the cold no more, I
               never felt such cold. This fuckin' country. How
               come you don't feel the cold?

EVANGELINE   Come on.

KEVIN   Take me home. I want to go home.

EVANGELINE   We have no home! You know that.

KEVIN   Then I'll go to fucking Millhaven. At least there's
               television there. Regular food.

EVANGELINE   Kevin. Kevin look at me.

KEVIN   (*he laughs*) What are you going to do, have the baby
               out here? In the bush? And then keep walkin' with
               her? What do you do when it's time to put her in
               school?

EVANGELINE   I have plans for Annie, Kevin. Annie will be just fine. Now can you please try to walk?

> *EVANGELINE decides to carry him. She lifts him over her shoulder. She sings to him, a Cree lullaby (see music for "Evangeline Carries Kevin" at end of play). She lifts him onto her back and they climb the hill where ANNIE was killed. KEVIN wakes, a final burst of energy before dying. He hears wolves.*

> *The Northern Lights light up the sky.*

KEVIN   Wha's that sound? 'Vangeline, it's the wolves. Oh yes. There they are. In the blizzard, can you see them?

EVANGELINE   Oh, no, my little brother. No! It's something else. Something kind. Yes. *Cheepyuk Neemeetowuk.* They've finally come for us. Oh. Dancing spirits. Yes. They're every bit as lovely as you said, Kev.

> *His breathing has become shallow, quick, as breathing often does before death. The Northern Lights surround them. ANNIE sings:*

ANNIE   Oh heavenly time of day...
the fog and the quiet.
The mist, no sun. I move out of my dream and into this day as
the fog it clears so slowly away to reveal.....to reveal...

> *The Snowy Owl hoots.*

> *The End.*

Michael Mahonen - KEVIN and Ron White - JACK.

— by Clylla von Tiedemann

Oh heavenly time of day

words by Judith Thompson
music by Bill Thompson

Thursday in November

words by Judith Thompson
music by Bill Thompson

Thursday in November at that duskish time of day

walk - ing west on Bloor street past Italian groceries Kor-

-ean fruit and flowers Hun - gar - i - an deli

I feel a sharp pain in my knee a red dog no a fox has

...ritardando...

bit - - ten me ...it's a fox... at Bloor & Bathurst my downtown

in the rushing a red fox is here and has bitten my knee and it

My mother and father

words by Judith Thompson
music by Bill Thompson

my

fa - - ther and mother are getting old

I and my brother were sad when they sold our old

house with its sagging porch and kitchen mouse and view of the forks of the

credit river we were puppies biting at their heels now they are

old don't finish their meals

saying goodbye to ghosts

my mother and father are getting

old

Morning in bright fall

words by Judith Thompson
music by Bill Thompson

Evangeline's Lament for Jack

Evangeline Carries Kevin

"Crowding Round Her":
Violence and Female Subjectivity

With *Sled*, Judith Thompson returns to a theme of her earlier plays: violence. In this play, as in the earlier work, violence forms — or perhaps more accurately, deforms — the lives of all the characters. In *Sled*, the violence unleashed by the play's initial murder (Kevin's killing of Annie) seems to gain force exponentially through the course of the dramatic action. By the end of the play, in a bold dramaturgical gesture reminiscent of classical tragedy, most of the characters have died violent deaths at Kevin's hand. Thompson is careful in her representation of violence, suggesting that violence and its effects are calibrated: the violence perpetuated by men renders the victims, in their final moments, as objects without humanity.

The first murder in *Sled*, the death of Annie, sets the context for the audience's understanding of subsequent murders. Annie is a lounge singer from Toronto who is performing at a lodge in Northern Ontario. Her husband Jack, a cop, has accompanied her, presumably in an attempt to work through tensions in the marriage. Asks Annie, "Is it working, Jack? ... You think things are going to be alright? With us?" Kevin and his friend Mike, in the area to hunt moose, are in the dining room having their dinner. They seem intent on being disruptively rowdy, taunting the owner of the lodge and then Annie. Says Mike, "Like, how you get so tall and skinny anyways? Did you, like, eat the CN tower?" Jack responds quickly, approaching the two young men, "Before you go any further, I would like you both to go down on your knees and apologise, to my wife, NOW."

The terms of the apology which Jack demands warrant consideration. He asks not simply for a apology, but for a demonstration of his power by the two young men acceding to his will through the staging of their contrition: Kevin and Mike must demonstrate their recognition of their wrongful behaviour by apologising on their knees. And, the apology is not to Annie, but to "my wife." Jack erases Annie by appropriating whatever humiliation she might have felt to demonstrate his power: he demands an apology because *his* wife has been offended. He wants the two young men to submit to his will. Annie simply serves as the currency in this exchange "between men," a phrase which I borrow from the title of Eve Sedgwick's book.

This scene is the catalyst for Kevin's revenge in which he shoots Jack's "possession" through the heart. Annie, who has woken early one morning, before dawn, decides to go for a walk through the woods. As she is walking, Kevin and Mike approach on snowmobiles (or "sleds") with engines roaring loudly. Kevin alerts Mike, who hasn't seen her, that their quarry is in sight. Drunk, adrenaline rushing at the prospect of the kill, the two approach. Annie begs, pleads that they take off their head phones, but they continue to stalk her as if her cries are unheard. Kevin speaks of her as if she were a moose, "Let's cut open her belly, and if there's a calf there, we pull out the calf."

As a member of the audience it is difficult not to feel revulsion at the unfolding scene in which Kevin stalks a woman whom he refuses to identify as human, instead seeing her as a pregnant cow whose calf will be wrenched from her belly. Annie pleads and pleads, but her voice isn't heard because the two wear headphones which drown out all sound except their own voices. Annie freezes in shock, like an animal caught in lights. She is without voice, without mobility, without agency. Kevin even refuses to acknowledge verbally that she is human. He shoots her "right through the heart," an image not only of killing her, but of destroying her capacity to love.

Mike, blind in one eye and unable to hear Annie's cries, doesn't realise that the quarry is human until he and Kevin approach the kill. Kevin is quite clear that he deliberately followed Annie as a means of "getting back at the cop." This murder is a response to Jack's demand that the two men apologize to Annie on bended knees. The gendered dynamic of the scene in which Jack demands an apology and the one in which Annie is shot are strikingly similar: in both Annie, as an individual with agency and voice, is diminished until she is the currency in an exchange between men.

At this point, it is worth noting the theatrical implications of the scene because Thompson seems to be playing with spectatorship. The theatre, given the root of the word in the Greek *theatron*, is the seeing place. In the contemporary theatre, the audience sits in the darkened house and watches the action on the illuminated stage. Watching the scene of Annie's murder, it is difficult not to note certain parallels between the scene being depicted and the position of the spectator watching the scene. The troubling question raised by the audience watching performers "caught" in stage light is: we may identify with Annie, but to what degree does our watching the performers parallel Kevin's relation to her?

The problem of seeing is a concern in *Sled*, a problem which, like violence, is gendered. If gender, of the roles assigned to men and to women occur within a complex network of social relations which are always inflected by power, and power within Western culture has rested with men, then the ways in which men and women watch, logically, are different. This difference is staged in *Sled* when Jack brings home an erotic video. Watching the video, both become aroused, with Jack offering a transparent justification of his arousal saying that he likes "the blonde" because she's a "good actress." The video, and the responses of Annie and Jack, are playful at this point. While smooching on the couch, Jack's attention periodically diverts from immediacy of their love-making to the action of the video. Annie realises the video is more arousing to him than she is. She is revolted and she asks that the video be turned off. Jack is perplexed by her response — "I thought you were enjoying it." There is a silence between them and then Annie, fully understanding the violence inherent even in a "gentle porno movie", says, "All those men, crowding round her..." Jack is perplexed by this, failing to understand that scene evokes a visceral response in Annie whose life, in a sense, appears to be about if not literal crowding, certainly metaphoric crowding round her. Certainly, the scene in the dining room of the lodge is a demonstration of men "crowding" out Annie's voice. A part of *Sled's* thematic project is an exploration of men "crowding" around women and the resulting negation of the female voice, the desires which it speaks and the fraught negotiation of the female subject to live in the face of this negation.

The problem of spectatorship in *Sled* takes on particular complexity for an audience because of the play's shifting theatrical styles which characterise Thompson's work. Critics of her earlier plays--and I would expect those studying *Sled*--cannot help but be drawn to her confident use of language which ranges between gritty, highly realistic exchanges between people and the poetic lyricism of the monologues given to individual characters. In the hands of a less-gifted playwright, these stylistic shifts might be jarringly abrupt, but in Thompson's work, they are seamless, a feature which has confounded critics who are intent placing her work within neat categories. Try as you might, if you assign the work to one stylistic category, it exceeds the boundaries of that style. This stylistic fluidity, a strength of the work, does present difficulties in discussing violence which might be seen as figurative and its actual impact on people transformed into metaphor. In *Sled*, Thompson deftly navigates the difficulties of representing violence: there are occasions in *Sled* when violence is not physical but psychological, and seems to approach the rhetorical status of metaphor, but Thompson insists that each instance of violence has damaging consequences for the character who is subjected to the violence. That some of the violence seems almost metaphoric creates a certain fragility around the violence in the play, because of the status of the script in theatre. A script is interpreted by practitioners who will stage the work within the materiality of theatre. In that translation, violence might easily become metaphor and its horrific consequences for the victims diminished, dismissed — dare I say, "crowded" out — simply a metaphor and not acts which damage.

As I mentioned, the sheer number of dead at the end of *Sled* suggests a force at work in this play akin to the notion of "fate" in classical drama. It might be that Kevin is "evil," that he is — to paraphrase Mike — in league with the devil. Certainly, the theological impulse so evident in Thompson's earlier work — for example, Isobel's forgiveness of her killer which precedes her ascent into heaven at the end of *Lion in the Streets* — has not been abandoned completely in *Sled*. Evangeline, Kevin's sister, prays "Hail Oh Hail Annie full of Grace we are soaked we are soaked in our neighbour's blood my brother and I the Law is with thee. Come to me I wait here. . . ." But in *Sled*, Thompson is not content to suggest that violence is a simple matter of "evil"; rather violence occurs within a social context, and so is an exercise of power which is related to issues of power and gender. In this context, it might be useful to draw the reader's attention to two other moments in the play and their implications.

Annie and Jack live in Seaton Village — the setting of *Lion in the Streets*. Thompson conveys a strong sense of the neighbourhood, one with a history of being home to immigrants. Across the street from Annie and Jack live a retired couple, Joe and Essie. Joe is the son of Italian immigrants. Among his strong memories of growing up is the day that his father was killed, shot by his own brother in the family home. The event not only traumatised Joe as a child, but disrupted profoundly the life of the family because his mother, now left as the sole support of the family, seems — at least in Joe's mind — to hold him responsible.

In the necessarily selective version of his personal history, Joe remembers Carmella, his mother, concerned with money and forcing him to wear her shoes to school. She "hits him hard. He cries and slowly puts the shoes on. He is totally humiliated ... His mother is very upset for him, but cannot show him." Tottering off to school in his mother's shoes, humiliated — both through her lashing out physically and then through Joe's having to wear her shoes, a visible index of the family's poverty — the scene has a further implication: Joe, in wearing those shoes, occupies a feminine position.

In the course of the play, through the force of "fate" which draws the seemingly unrelated lives of these individuals together, Kevin is reunited with his sister Evangeline. We learn that Kevin, as a young child, was stolen from the family by his baby-sitter and raised in Northern Ontario. Kevin, after killing Annie, seeks refuge with Evangeline who is the next-door neighbour of Joe and Essie. On a fateful evening, Kevin encounters his sister in the company of Jack and the two face off, Jack initially not recognising Kevin and defending Evangeline's right to date whomever she pleases when Kevin forbids her to see Jack (a move hauntingly reminiscent of his defence of Annie's honour.) The two interact through violence. Jack pursues Kevin into the house where he finds the dress Annie had been wearing when she was murdered. He realises that he is facing his wife's killer and is intent on avenging her death. He wrestles Kevin, pinning him in a strangle hold which forces Evangeline to make a choice which renders her, whatever her choice, complicit in a man's death. She takes a gun and kills Jack.

This is an important moment in the play because, unlike Kevin's killing of Annie in which he sees his victim as an animal, Evangeline makes a choice between complicity in her brother's death or in killing the man who is killing her brother. Her action makes evident that Thompson depicts violence as calibrated and gendered. Like Carmella who hits her son, Evangeline never loses sight that hers is act of violence against another person. Kevin insistently reduces his victims: first in the killing of Annie, then later, in the killing of Mike whom he can't allow to live because he is a witness. Like Jack's act of pinning Kevin to the floor, Kevin's acts of violence are defined by his refusing his victims mobility and voice.

Conventionally, violence is represented by dramatists as having such force that it annihilates. Certainly, in *Sled*, violence shatters individuals and their sense of personal identity — witness Joe's vivid memories in old age of his father's death, an event which forever changed his sense of himself. But violence is incorporated into the weave of a community's history: Joe's story is part of the fabric of the neighbourhood's history because it is part of his personal history. The bold, and perhaps unpalatable, suggestion in *Sled* is that violence doesn't shatter a community, but is incorporated into its identity. All the dead in *Sled* continue to be presences — albeit ghostly ones — within the community. In praying to Annie, Evangeline is not simply expressing a need for forgiveness, but appealing to the presence of the dead. For Thompson, the dead — whose voices are crowded out and unheard — are vitally present. These voices need to be heard, particularly the voices which were not heard in life. Annie is a victim of a mode of masculinity which systematically erased her; should we perpetuate the violence of that erasure by refusing to be attentive to her ghostly presence? She, and those like her, are part of the fabric of our community, whether community is understood on the local level of the neighbourhood or as that community called nation.

Ann Wilson
Department of Drama
University of Guelph
February, 1997

Other plays by Judith Thompson

Lion in the Streets
Playwrights Canada Press
ISBN 0-88754-515-7
$10.95

White Biting Dog
Playwrights Canada Press
ISBN 0-88754-369-3
$10.95

The Other Side of the Dark:
    I Am Yours
    The Crackwalker
    Pink
    Tornado
Playwrights Canada Press
ISBN 0-88754-537-8
$19.95

Catalogues & Theatre Communications Group publications...

Telephone, fax, write, or e-mail for a complete Playwrights Canada
Press catalogue from Canada's award-winning drama publisher.
Playwrights Canada Press is also the exclusive distributor in Canada of
the entire list of drama and theatre titles published by Theatre
Communications Group in New York, including *Angels in America* by
Tony Kushner, and the plays of Caryl Churchill, Stephen Sondheim,
and Athol Fugard among many others.

Also, for the complete Playwrights Union of Canada catalogue of more
than 1500 Canadian plays in all formats: trade paperbacks from many
different publishers, chapbooks, playscripts, and copyscripts, send $5.00
(shipping and handling) to the address below.

Playwrights Canada Press / Playwrights Union of Canada
54 Wolseley St., 2nd fl., Toronto ON M5T 1A5
tel: (416) 703-0201 / fax: 703-0059
cdplays@interlog.com
http://www.puc.ca